ENERGY
LAB
FOR KIDS

40 EXCITING
EXPERIMENTS TO
EXPLORE, CREATE, HARNESS,
AND UNLEASH ENERGY

ENERGY
LAB
for Kids

EMILY HAWBAKER

and

THE NEED PROJECT

QUARRY

Quarto is the authority on a wide range of topics.

Quarto educates, entertains and enriches the lives of our readers—enthusiasts and lovers of hands-on living.

www.QuartoKnows.com

First published in the United States of America in 2017 by
Quarry Books, an imprint of
Quarto Publishing Group USA Inc.
100 Cummings Center
Suite 265-D
Beverly, Massachusetts 01915-6101
Telephone: (978) 282-9590
Fax: (978) 283-2742
QuartoKnows.com
Visit our blogs at QuartoKnows.com

10 9 8 7 6 5 4 3 2 1

ISBN: 978-1-63159-250-8

Digital edition published in 2017

Library of Congress Cataloging-in-Publication Data available

Design: Samantha J. Bednarek
Photography: Amber Procaccini Photography // www.aprocciniphoto.com
Photography Styling: Liz Lee Heinecke // www.kitchenpantryscientist.com

Printed in China

The information in this book is for educational purposes only.

DEDICATED TO THE STUDENTS WHO INSPIRE US EACH DAY.

CONTENTS

UNIT 05

SAVING ENERGY

FOREWORD

BY LIZ HEINEKE

RECENTLY, I ASKED SOME KIDS why they think it's important to understand the science of energy. Here is what they told me.

James: "So that we can learn how to power the world without using up all our natural resources."

Oliver: "So we can learn about our impact on Earth."

Lily: "So we can understand that driving is bad for the environment and that things like riding my bike can help."

Sarah: "Because lots of stuff has energy."

I learned a thing or two about energy science, myself, when I joined photographer Amber Procaccini and a troop of smart, funny kids to experiment our way through the labs in this book.

Some of these labs are instant, science fair–worthy, hits. Kids will discover it's simple to create an electro-magnet using doorbell wire, a 9–volt battery, a nail, and some paper clips. Making glow sticks glow even brighter by putting them in hot water is a fun way to show how thermal energy can speed up chemical reactions. And, burning cheese puffs in a homemade calorimeter is an exciting (and smelly) way to measure the energy in food.

I was also impressed by how well many labs illustrate the conservation issues surrounding natural resources. For example, the Chocolate Chip Extraction Competition (see page 54) demonstrates the difficulty of restoring something to its original state after you tear it apart, whether you're mining for chocolate or copper.

In science, the journey is as important as the result. Teaching kids the importance of mistakes, innovation, and persistence is crucial to raising creative thinkers. Lighting a bulb with aluminum foil and a battery re-quired a few tries, but the kids' eyes shone even brighter than the bulbs when they succeeded. And although the magnetic generator didn't work on the first try, think-ing about why it wasn't working and troubleshooting the problem allowed the kids to really understand the science behind the fun.

As we wrapped up our lab experiments, I asked *Energy Lab for Kids* author Emily Hawbaker why she thinks we should understand more about energy. She said, "Almost everything we do requires energy. We use more and more of it each year across the globe as we become more tech savvy, but much of the energy we use around the world comes from nonrenewable resources that have a limited supply. Understanding how we use energy and how we can be more responsible with it is important to making sure that future generations have energy that is sustain-able and meets their demands."

Naturally, her answer was more eloquent than those of the kids, but it was remarkably similar to their combined responses. I look forward to the future, as today's kids become tomorrow's inventors and find new ways to use energy more efficiently and less destructively, creating a better tomorrow for us all.

Liz Heineke is the author of Kitchen Science Lab for Kids. *A molecular biologist by training, Liz's love of shar-ing science with her three children led to her developing her website KitchenPantryScientist. She serves as an Earth Ambassador for NASA. Liz works to make it sim-ple for parents to do science with kids of all ages and for kids to experiment safely on their own.*

INTRODUCTION

ENERGY IS ALL AROUND US. We hear about it on the news, we use it every day, and sometimes we're even told we have too much energy. But what *is* energy? Have you ever plugged a device into the wall and thought about where that electricity comes from? It isn't magic that allows us to flip a switch and turn on the lights or fill our gas tank and make our cars and buses move—it's energy and it's science.

This book is meant for everyone! The lab activities will help you explore almost everything about energy—what it is, how we find it, how we use it, and how we can save it. Many of the labs use familiar science-process skills, such as making predictions and observations, taking measurements, and drawing conclusions. And while all of the labs are written for kids, they're fun for adults, too.

WHAT WILL YOU NEED?

Nearly all of the supplies used in this book are things you're likely to find around the house or in a local store. If you have something on hand that's slightly different than an item on a lab's materials list, go ahead and try it. It might work! It can't hurt to experiment—that's what labs are all about! If there are materials you have trouble finding, check out the list of resources provided on page 134.

Most of the labs can be done indoors on a flat work surface, preferably near a kitchen for easy cleanup. Clear off a space on your counter or table. A plastic tablecloth or newspaper might also come in handy to protect the surface. If a lab could get messy or works better outdoors, we will warn you at the beginning of the activity.

SAFETY IS KEY

All of the labs are safe to complete in a home setting using common materials. However, if you have safety goggles, we suggest you wear them! When working through science experiments, follow any warnings you might see and pay attention to safety procedures.

TIME AND PERSON POWER

At the start of each lab, note the amount of time it should take to complete the experiment. Most can be completed in an hour or less, but a few require monitoring or measuring over a series of hours or days.

Some of the activities are simple and can be completed by one person from start to finish. Others are more complex and require supervision or an additional pair of hands. The label "No Sweat!" means that the lab has easy set-up and cleanup and can be completed alone. "Grab a Crew Member!" tells you that a lab might require some supervision or an extra pair of hands. "All Hands on Deck!" means the lab is trickier and will be more effective with a few friends or family members.

Have fun and get energized!

—Emily Hawbaker

 Check under this symbol at the start of each lab to find out about the time, person power, mess alert, and safety.

UNIT 01

ENERGY BASICS

WHAT IS ENERGY? You've probably heard someone describe another person as "high energy," or perhaps you've seen a news story about clean energy. Energy is all around us: it's a part of everything we do and everything we see. It can be described as the ability to do work or make a change. It helps people move and plants grow. It powers machines and technology. We observe energy all around us in the forms of heat, light, sound, and motion.

The labs in this unit will help you recognize that energy is always present. By the end of Unit 1, you'll be able to observe many of the things energy can do. You will explore how heat moves in solids, liquids, and gases. You'll observe light and how it travels. You'll test how objects move with different amounts of energy and friction. You'll make sound travel through different mediums. These are all examples of work or change.

Let's get to work!

Observing convection currents in Lab 1.

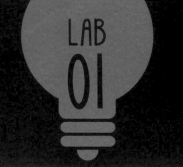
CONVECTION CURRENT IN A CUP

TIME:
15 minutes

PERSON POWER:
No Sweat!

MESS ALERT!
Be cautious with food coloring; it can stain fabrics, furnishings, and your skin. Use a plastic tablecloth or newspaper under the cups, just in case!

SAFETY IS KEY:
Be cautious handling hot water. The hot water needed for this activity should be just under boiling, approximately 185–200°F (85–93°C). Use the cooking thermometer to check the temperature.

Why does the deep end of a pool always feel so much colder? Why does cold coffee creamer sink to the bottom of a cup of hot coffee, so that it needs to be stirred? This lab will explore how heat, or thermal energy, moves through fluids.

MATERIALS

→ **2 clear plastic cups per color**
→ **cold water**
→ **food coloring**
→ **4 or 5 marbles**
→ **hot water**
→ **cooking or lab thermometer**

1. Fill one plastic cup ¾ full with cold water.

2. Wait until the water has become completely still.

3. Add a few drops of food coloring (fig. 1). What happens to the food coloring? Take a photograph or draw a picture of what you see.

4. Empty the cup.

Fig. 1: Add a few drops of food coloring.

5. Put the marbles in the bottom of the second cup.

6. Add hot water to the cup so that the hot water just covers the marbles (fig. 2).

7. Put the first cup on top of the marbles and hot water (fig. 3). Fill this cup with cold water again.

8. Add a few drops of food coloring to the cold water (fig. 4). What happens to the food coloring this time? Take a few photographs or a video, or draw a picture of what you see happening over time (fig. 5).

Fig. 2: Add hot water to cover the marbles in the cup.

Fig. 3: Put the first cup on top of the marbles and hot water.

Fig. 4: Add a few drops of food coloring to the cold water.

Fig. 5: Take photographs of what you see.

Heat Seesaw

Everything in nature seeks balance. Heat seeks balance, too. Heat flows from high temperature to low temperature. What happens if you pour hot water into a cold tub? The molecules of hot water are moving fast and will have more energy. These hot water molecules crash and collide into the colder molecules, giving them some of their energy. The hot water molecules slow down, having lost some energy, while the colder molecules start to speed up. The cold water becomes warmer, and the hot water gets cooler. This continues until all the water is the same temperature and all the water molecules are moving at the same speed. It's like the hot and cold molecules are on a seesaw!

This seesaw happens in all substances: solids, liquids, and gases!

You just observed heat—but what is it? Heat is the motion of molecules in a substance. The substance itself is not moving, but its molecules are constantly in motion. This motion is thermal energy, or heat. Heat always moves from areas of high temperature (high energy), to areas of low temperature (lower energy), until the temperatures equalize.

Liquids, like water, and gases, like air, are classified as fluids. Heat moves through fluids in a process called convection. In this lab, you created a convection current in your cup: When a fluid is heated, the warmer parts of the fluid become less dense and float to the top. Cooler fluids are denser than warmer fluids, so while the warm fluid floats to the top, the cool fluid sinks to the bottom. This cycle continues until the temperature of the fluid begins to equalize. In your cup, this may only take a few minutes, but in larger spaces or in nature, it can take a very long time.

BEACH BASICS

TIME:
30 minutes or more

PERSON POWER:
No Sweat!

SAFETY IS KEY:
Be cautious when handling lightbulbs, as they may become hot when illuminated.

Sometimes on a hot day at the beach, you have to run from your blanket to the water. That sand is *so* hot! Why is the sand so much hotter than the water? And why, on a summer night, is the sand cooler than the water? This lab explores how heat, or thermal energy, can travel and be absorbed by substances. Do different substances absorb and hold their thermal energy differently?

Fig. 3: Put a thermometer into each cup.

Figs. 1 and 2: Fill one cup with water and the second cup with sand.

Much of the Earth's energy comes from the sun in rays or waves called radiant energy. When the sun's radiant energy radiates toward the Earth, it hits molecules in the ocean, on land, in our bodies, and in the air. Those molecules turn some of this energy into heat. You're creating a mini version of this process using your lamp. The heat (thermal energy) from the lamp radiated into the cups. The sand will heat up more quickly than water. However, when the lamp is turned off, the water probably stayed warmer longer than the sand. This is very much like what we experience during a day at the beach.

Some materials are able to absorb and release heat faster than others. Sand is one of these materials.

MATERIALS

→ 2 clear plastic cups
→ 2 cooking or lab thermometers
→ room-temperature sand
→ room-temperature water
→ timer
→ desk lamp with heat bulb or traditional incandescent bulb

1. Fill one cup with water (fig. 1).

2. Fill the second cup with sand so the sand and water are at the same level (fig. 2).

3. Put a thermometer into each cup (fig. 3). Record the starting temperature of each cup. Make a table like the one on page 19 to record your data.

4. Place both cups about 4" (10 cm) away from the lamp (fig. 4). Turn on the lamp. Make sure that both cups are receiving approximately the same amount of light.

LAB
02

BEACH BASICS

What a Breeze!

Wind is energy in motion, but where does it come from? As you learned in this lab, when the sun shines, land warms faster than water. Land absorbs energy from the sun quickly and changes it to heat. This means that the air just above the land will also be warmer than the air above the water. Warm air over the land rises and moves out toward the ocean, where it cools and sinks toward the water. When it does, the cooler ocean air moves in toward land. This is called a sea breeze—the refreshing, cool air from the sea. Overnight, however, this process reverses. Why? Think about what you observed in this lab. At night, the land cools more quickly than water. Since the ocean retains its temperature longer, the air above it stays warmer. Warm air rises up from the ocean and sinks down again when it reaches the land. The cooler land air rushes out to sea. This is called a land breeze. The movement of air in this fashion is what creates wind!

Fig. 4: Place both cups about 4" (10 cm) away from the lamp.

Fig. 5: Record the temperature every minute for ten minutes

5. Set a timer for one minute and record the temperature in each cup every minute for ten minutes. Does one material have a higher temperature? Why?

6. Turn off the lamp and record the temperature every minute for ten minutes (fig. 5). Did one material cool more quickly?

NOW TRY This!

Different materials absorb and retain heat in different ways. Does color or texture matter, too? Experiment by filling cups with different colors of sand and water and repeat the steps of the lab. Try it with cups of different materials like rocks or even a cup of air!

— **DID YOU KNOW?** —

At the beach, you'll need less bug spray during the day than you will at night. Why? Because of the direction of the breeze! Fewer bugs hang out over the ocean, so when there's a sea breeze there are fewer bugs to bite you!

BEACH BASICS DATA

TIME	LAMP		NO LAMP	
	Sand	Water	Sand	Water
Starting				
1 min				
2 mins				
3 mins				
4 mins				
5 mins				
6 mins				
7 mins				
8 mins				
9 mins				
10 mins				

WHAT A GAS!

LAB 03

PERSON POWER:
Grab a Crew Member!
It might be handy to
have help tying the
balloon and holding it
for measurements.

SAFETY IS KEY:
Use caution with the
hot water. The hot water
needed for this activity
should be just under
boiling, approximately
185–200°F (85–93°C).
Use tongs or an oven
mitt to place your
balloon in the hot water.

We know that heat, or thermal energy, travels through solids and liquids well. But what happens when it travels through gases like air, oxygen, or helium? In this lab, we'll trap some gas from our lungs (breath!) in a balloon and explore what happens when it's heated or cooled.

MATERIALS

→ 1 or 2 round balloons
→ bowl of ice water
→ bowl of hot water
→ measuring tape
→ oven mitt or tongs
→ cooking or lab thermometer

1. Blow up the balloon to the size of a baseball and tie it (fig. 1).

2. Allow the balloon to sit for a few minutes so that the gas in the balloon can equalize with the temperature of the room.

3. Use the measuring tape to measure the circumference of the balloon at its widest point (fig. 2). Circumference is the distance around a circular object.

Fig. 4: Carefully put the balloon in the hot water for one minute.

4. Check the temperature of the room using your thermometer. Keep in mind the size of your balloon at this temperature, or take a picture of it!

5. Fill a bowl with ice water. Place the balloon in the ice water for one minute (fig. 3). After one minute, measure the circumference of the balloon and the temperature of the water. Did you notice a change?

6. Fill a bowl with hot water. Using tongs or an oven mitt, carefully put the balloon in the hot water for one minute (fig. 4). After one minute, measure the circumference of the balloon and the temperature of the hot water. Did you notice a change?

Fig. 1: Blow up the balloon to the size of a baseball.

Fig. 2: Measure the circumference of the balloon.

Fig. 3: Place the balloon in the ice water for one minute.

Don't Step on a Crack!

Ever wonder why sidewalks become cracked? All materials expand when they're heated and contract when they're cooled. When sidewalks and roads heat up and cool down as the seasons change, they expand and contract, too, which can cause cracks. When sidewalks and roads are designed with seams or joints between sections, the surfaces can expand and contract without cracking.

Now Try This!

Perform the experiment again, but this time, use a kitchen scale to take the mass of the balloon at the start and again after you take the balloon out of the hot and cold water. When the balloon changes size, does it change its mass? Mass is a measure of the amount of matter—has the amount of matter in the balloon changed?

Use a kitchen scale to take the mass of the balloon.

ENERGY EXPLAINED

When thermal energy (heat) is applied to a substance, its molecules move faster and push apart from each other. The spaces between the molecules become greater. When you put your balloon in hot water, it got bigger. The molecules of your breath stayed the same size inside the balloon but moved more rapidly and pushed apart, causing the balloon to expand. The opposite occurred when you put the balloon in the ice water. As heat energy is taken away, molecules slow down and move closer together, causing the balloon to shrink!

All substances expand when they're heated—solids, liquids, and gases! Some expand a little and some expand a lot.

SHADOW SHAPER

Fig. 2: Place the flashlight 12" (30 cm) from the paper.

TIME:
15–20 minutes

PERSON POWER:
No Sweat!

We use light energy every day. Light that we see is called visible light, and it travels like waves in straight lines. But light can't pass through most objects. This lab will explore how shadows are created when something blocks light's path.

MATERIALS

→ 11" x 17" (28 x 43 cm) piece of white paper
→ tape
→ table or flat surface near a wall
→ flashlight, (single bulb, non-LED works best)
→ small object, such as a wooden spool or nail polish bottle
→ ruler
→ notebook and pencil

1. Tape the paper vertically on the wall closest to the table (fig. 1). The bottom edge of the paper should be at the same level as the table top.

2. Place the flashlight on the table 12" (30 cm) from the paper (fig. 2). Orient the bulb so that the light points at the paper.

3. Measure the height of the small object (fig. 3). Record the height so you remember it later. Draw a table like the one on page 25, if necessary.

4. Position the small object between the flashlight and the paper, so that the middle of the object is 2" (5 cm) from the paper on the wall.

5. Measure the height of the shadow. Notice how clear or blurry the shadow and its edges appear. How does the height of the shadow compare to the height of the object? Record your observations on the chart.

Fig. 1: Tape the paper vertically on the wall.

Light energy travels in waves called radiant energy. We call the light we see "visible" light, because we can't see the actual light waves. What we see is the reflection of light off substances. Not all radiant energy can be detected by the eye. Radio waves, X-rays, and cell phone signals also travel as radiant energy that can be detected by special devices.

Our eyes are a special instrument for detecting light. We see objects only because light waves are reflected off an object and into our eyes.

Light waves travel in straight lines and do not change direction unless they are reflected or refracted (bent). When light hits the wooden spool, for example, it cannot pass through or go around it. The spool blocks the light from reaching the wall and an area without light is created. We call the areas without light "shadows."

As you move an item closer to a light source, its shadow appears larger because the object is blocking more light. As you move the item further away from the light source, the shadow becomes smaller and sharper because the object is blocking less light.

SUNDIAL

Early Egyptians knew all about shadows and how light travels. They observed that the sun follows the same pattern in the sky each day. They realized that as the position of the sun changes in the sky, so does your shadow. They used their observations to create a tool for telling time. This device, a sundial, was made simply by placing a stick in the ground. They used the length and position of the shadow to tell them the time of day!

Fig. 4: How does the shadow change with each movement of the object?

6. Move the object back so that it is 4" (10 cm) from the paper on the wall. How has the shadow changed?

7. Continue moving the object closer to the flashlight, at distances of 6", 8", and 10" (15, 20, and 25 cm) from the wall. How does the shadow change with each movement of the object (fig. 4)?

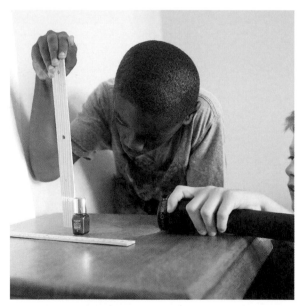

Fig. 3: How does the shadow change with each movement of the object?

NOW TRY THIS!

Hold the flashlight at a different angle. How does your object's shadow change? Have some time on your hands? Go outside on a sunny day and have a friend take a picture of your shadow. Mark the spot where you stood, and come back to repeat this process every hour for a few hours. How does your shadow change and why? Come back to the spot a few months later at approximately the same times. Does your shadow change?

SHADOW SHAPER DATA

FLASHLIGHT DISTANCE TO WALL	OBJECT DISTANCE TO WALL	SHADOW HEIGHT	SHADOW CLARITY
12 inches (30 cm)	2 inches (5 cm)		
12 inches (30 cm)	4 inches (10 cm)		
12 inches (30 cm)	6 inches (15 cm)		
12 inches (30 cm)	8 inches (20 cm)		
12 inches (30 cm)	10 inches (25 cm)		

LAB 05

MIRROR MADNESS

When light strikes an object, it can pass through the object, be absorbed by the object, or be reflected by the object. This lab will explore how light can bounce off an object in a straight line. You'll be making your own fun house of mirrors!

TIME:
30 minutes

PERSON POWER:
If you have nine stuffed toys, you can do this activity by yourself or with the help of a friend. Otherwise, grab nine crew members, because it's All Hands on Deck!

SAFETY IS KEY:
This activity requires a full-length mirror. Ask for help from an adult to move and orient your mirror for the lab. Mirrors can be heavy and are breakable. Be careful when you move mirrors, especially if you're superstitious!

Fig. 5: All the toys should be in a straight line.

MATERIALS

→ full-length mirror
→ measuring tape
→ 9 stuffed toys (or friends)
→ sticky labels
→ colored pencils
→ paper
→ protractor

1. Place the mirror vertically against a wall. Hang or place it on top of a few stacked books, so that it is 8" (20 cm) off the floor (fig. 1).

2. Make labels for your nine stuffed toys (or friends), each one with a number 1 to 9 (fig. 2).

3. Position toy 5 so it is 60" (1.5 m) from the center of the mirror (fig. 3).

4. Position toys 1 through 4 to the left of toy 5 (fig. 4), each one 16" (41 cm) away from the next. Do the same with toys 6 through 9 on the right. All the toys should be in a straight line, 60" (1.5 m) from the mirror wall (fig. 5).

5. Draw a diagram of the mirror and the toys.

6. Stand directly behind toy 1, kneel to its level, and look directly into the mirror (fig. 6). Which toys can you see? On your diagram, draw a straight line with a colored pencil from toy 1 to the mirror and from the mirror to any toy you see.

7. Stand directly behind toy 2. Using a different color, repeat step 6 and draw your lines. Repeat this for all nine toys.

8. Use a protractor to measure the angles you drew.

Fig. 1: Place the mirror so that it is 8" (20 cm) off the floor.

Fig. 2: Make labels for your stuffed toys (or friends).

Fig. 3: Position toy 5 so it is 60" (1.5 m) from the mirror.

Fig. 4: Position toys 1 through 4 to the left of toy number 5.

Fig. 6: Stand behind toy 1 and kneel to its level.

ENERGY EXPLAINED

We see light waves that bounce off things—the light that is reflected. When you look at the person next to you or at your image in a mirror, you're seeing reflected light waves! In this lab, you're seeing light reflected off the stuffed toys. Some light waves travel toward the mirror and the mirror reflects them. Some of the waves from the mirror make it to your eyes.

Light waves are reflected at predictable angles. It's very much like when you bounce a ball. If you drop the ball straight down, it is going to bounce straight back up, not left or right. Light waves move the same way. When light waves hit an object, they reflect back at the same angle, in a straight line.

TO Reflect OR to Absorb?

Light waves can be reflected by mirrors, but reflection happens even if an item isn't shiny. Different materials reflect light differently based on their color, texture, and other properties. Light waves (radiant energy) can also enter a substance and change into other forms of energy. Our skin absorbs light energy and turns it into heat (thermal energy). Some things are better reflectors than others in nature. Snow and ice reflect light better than forests. Glass buildings and homes with light-colored paint reflect more light than a home made of stone or painted with dark colors.

RAMP IT UP!

Fig. 3: Repeat the trials, adding a book each time.

TIME:
20 minutes

PERSON POWER:
Grab a Crew Member! It's easier to have help finding your marble if it goes missing!

When you look around you, many things may be in motion. All of this motion takes energy; nothing can move without it. In this lab, you'll use ramps and marbles to explore the basics of motion and energy: What gets things moving, keeps things moving, and what makes things stop moving.

MATERIALS

→ 5 books (all the same thickness)
→ ruler with a grooved center channel
→ pencil and paper or notebook
→ marble
→ measuring tape or meter/ yardstick

1. Place one book on the floor (a smooth floor works best). Put the end of the ruler on the edge of the book binding and allow the ruler to extend out like a ramp.

2. On a piece of scrap paper or in a notebook, create a data table like the one on the right.

3. Place the marble at the top of the ruler and let it go. Let it roll down the ramp (fig. 1). Don't push it!

RAMP IT UP DATA

RAMP HEIGHT	TRIAL 1	TRIAL 2	TRIAL 3	TRIAL 4
1 Book				
2 Books				
3 Books				
4 Books				
5 Books				

Fig. 1: Place the marble at the top of the ruler and let it go.

Fig. 2: Stretch the measuring tape from the ruler ramp to the marble.

NOW TRY THiS!

Try the experiment on different surfaces, such as carpet, a wooden deck, grass, or asphalt.

Fig. 4: Repeat the trials until your ramp is five books high.

4. Allow the marble to come to a stop. Stretch the measuring tape from the bottom of the ruler ramp to the marble to see how far the marble traveled (fig. 2).

5. Record the distance and repeat two more times for a total of three trials. Calculate the average distance traveled for the marble at a ramp height of one book.

6. Repeat the trials, adding a book each time, until your ramp is five books high (figs. 3 and 4). How did the height of the ramp affect the marble's motion?

ENERGY EXPLAINED

All moving objects have energy. If an object isn't moving, it's storing energy until it is made to move. Your marble on the top of the ramp has energy. It's not moving, but it has the potential to move. We call this potential energy. But if you didn't give your marble a push, how does it get rolling?

Three hundred years ago, a famous guy you may have heard of, Sir Isaac Newton, figured out some major patterns related to motion. We call these Newton's Laws of Motion. Newton's first law states that in order for an object to move, a force must act upon it to make it move. It also states that a moving object will keep moving until a force acts on it to make it stop.

In the case of your marble, what makes it begin to move is a force called gravity. Gravity pulls things toward the ground and is what gives an object its potential energy. Height can affect the force of gravity on an object: the higher the object is from the ground, the more force it will have coming down. Your marble probably rolled farther, and maybe even faster, when the ramp was higher.

But what made your marble stop? It probably slowed to a stop. Why? As the marble rolls on the floor, it's making contact with air and the floor's surface. Both of those items push back against it, slowing it as it rolls and creating heat, just as if you rubbed your hands against one another. This force is called friction. Different surfaces contribute differently to friction. Did you ever go skating on the kitchen floor with your socks on? It just doesn't work the same way on carpet, because carpet is a high-friction surface. Using a smooth, flat table will keep your marble rolling longer than a surface like carpet or grass.

PENDULUM SWINGER

Fig. 3: Raise the washer to the side so that the string is taut.

TIME:
30 minutes

PERSON POWER:
All Hands on Deck! This activity works best with a few friends: one to work the stopwatch, one to do the swinging, and one to do the counting.

Motion doesn't always happen in a perfectly straight line. For example, if you get on the swings at a playground, why does the swing follow a curved path? Swings are examples of pendulums, and this lab sets up a mini pendulum to explore how gravity and motion work together.

MATERIALS

→ meter/yardstick
→ 2 tables or desks of the same height
→ piece of string, 2' long (61 cm)
→ several large ½" (1.3 cm) washers
→ stopwatch
→ measuring tape
→ masking tape

1. Place the yardstick across the two tables or desks.

2. Tie one washer to the end of the string.

3. Tie a loop at the other end of the string. Slide the loop onto the yardstick so that the washer hangs between the tables (fig. 1). Tape the loop in place on the yardstick, and tape the yardstick to the tables (fig. 2).

4. Raise the washer to the side so that the string is taut and the washer is at the same height as the yardstick (fig. 3).

5. Set your stopwatch for ten seconds.

6. Let the washer go, allowing it to swing back and forth (fig. 4). Count each complete back and forth motion the washer makes in ten seconds. Each back and forth is called one vibration. Make a table or chart to keep track, if needed.

Fig. 1: Tie a loop in the string and tie it onto the yardstick.

Fig. 2: Tape the loop into place.

Fig. 4: Let the washer go, allowing it to swing.

7. Remove the tape and slide the string off the yardstick. From the top, slide another washer down the string so it rests on the first washer. Reattach the string to the yardstick and tape it back into place so the washers hang between the tables.

8. Repeat steps 4 to 6. Do you see a difference? Add another washer or two and repeat. What do you observe?

9. Now try changing the height where you release your washer. Do you notice a difference?

NOW TRY THiS!

Try the experiment again with one washer. This time, however, shorten the string by half the length. Do you think the vibrations will increase or decrease? Continue adding washers each time and compare.

ENERGY EXPLAINED

All objects experience the force of gravity. When possible objects in motion move in a straight path. In the case of the pendulum, the object doesn't move in a straight line, it moves in a curved path. Why?

The pendulum is anchored at the top. The yardstick holds the string at a center point, and a force called centripetal force pulls the pendulum upward when you let go. Gravity and centripetal force work together, pulling in opposite directions, to make the pendulum swing back and forth in a curved path.

You probably didn't see much change in the vibrations when you added extra washers, increasing the mass. Mass does not affect a pendulum's swing. However, you will see a big difference in the vibration when you change the height of the pendulum's release. The higher you hold the washer, the longer it takes it to go back and forth.

SLINKY WAVES

Fig. 2: The motion should mimic the waves of the ocean.

PERSON POWER:
Grab a Crew Member! You'll need a partner or two to complete this activity.

Sound is energy. It travels in waves, but these waves are different than the waves that carry light, X-rays, radio signals, or even water. This lab explores the different types of wave motion to understand how sound energy is carried from one place to another.

MATERIALS

→ Slinky spring
→ long table

1. Your partner should stand across from you, holding one end of the spring, while you hold the other end (fig. 1). Another friend can record a video of the activity. It's really fun to view this in slow motion!

2. Your partner's end of the spring should be completely still while you move your end up and down slowly, about 4" (10 cm) off the surface. The motion should mimic ocean waves (fig. 2).

3. Move the spring more quickly, but at the same height. Does it respond in the same way?

4. Slow the movement down again, but increase the height to 8" (20 cm) off the surface (fig. 3). Observe the spring motion compared to the lower height, and then move it more quickly as in step 3. Has anything changed?

5. Now your partner should move the spring while you keep your end still (fig. 4).

6. Have your partner slowly push and pull the spring 6" (15 cm) forward and backward on the surface in a straight line, toward you. How does the spring respond this time?

7. Increase the speed of the forward and backward motion and observe. What happens when you increase the length of movement to 12" (30 cm)?

Fig. 1: Your partner should hold one end of the spring.

Fig. 3: Slow the movement down, but increase the height of the spring.

Fig. 4: Keep your end of the spring still while your partner moves the other end.

ENERGY EXPLAINED

Energy can travel in waves. Not all energy waves travel in the same manner. Ocean waves, visible light, and X-rays travel in an up and down motion. This is what you observed in the first half of the activity. When you moved the spring up and down on your end, the wave traveled forward.

Sound waves move differently. Sounds are caused by energy vibrating through things or by molecules moving back and forth. The molecules collide and pass on their energy in the same direction as the sound. You demonstrated this with the spring in the second half of the lab. As the spring is pushed forward, each piece pushes into the next piece, moving the energy forward, too. This is often called a longitudinal wave because it moves in one long line.

You can often feel the vibrations of sounds moving through you! Have you ever been to a loud concert or sporting event where you could feel the vibration as music thumped loudly? Place your fingers on your throat and hum a tune. Can you feel the vibration? Sound can vibrate and push its energy through liquids, gases, and solids, too. Energy, such as light, that travels in an up and down pattern is often stopped by a solid barrier.

NOW TRY THIS!

Explore the amplification of sound by inserting the bottom of a foam cup into a metal slinky. Hold the slinky up by your head and bounce it straight down to the ground and back. Then try holding it closer to the ground and bouncing it. What do you observe?

LAB 09

SOUND STOPPER

TIME:
30 minutes

PERSON POWER:
Grab a Crew Member! You'll need a partner or two for this activity. You'll take turns listening.

Sound waves travel in long lines and vibrate through materials. So, what makes a room soundproof? Often we can hear sounds through thick and heavy-duty materials. Will a material stop sound? This lab explores how sounds vibrate through various solids.

📎 MATERIALS

→ **smartphone with your favorite song downloaded**
→ **piece of paper**
→ **sweatshirt**
→ **cookie sheet**
→ **roll of paper towels**

1. Sit facing your partner, about 3' (91 cm) from each other. Place your materials between the two of you.

2. Hold the phone so that its speaker is aimed toward your partner. Press "play" on your song, and then place the paper so that it's between the speaker and your partner (fig. 1). It should be close to the speaker, but not touching it. Ask your partners to tell you what they observe about the song before and after you move the

Fig. 1: The motion should mimic the waves of the ocean.

paper into place. Do you notice anything different about the song on your side of the paper?

3. Keep the volume the same on your phone, start the song again, and repeat the process with the sweatshirt, cookie sheet, and roll of paper towels. Discuss what you hear each time with each item.

4. Switch roles and repeat (figs. 2–4).

5. Try substituting any type of barrier you wish! What items are great at stopping the sound? What items amplify the sound?

Figs. 2–4: Repeat the process with the sweatshirt, the cookie sheet, and the roll of paper towels.

Blind as a Bat

If you've ever heard this phrase, you'll know that bats have poor eyesight. Bats actually use sound waves to help them "see" while flying. Bats can tell where objects are by listening to how sounds are reflected. They emit a sound that travels out and then back to them. If sounds are reflected quickly, they know to change direction. Bats can even find the insects they feast on using sound waves!

ENERGY EXPLAINED

Sound waves move through the air in a straight line. When sound reaches an object, just like light, it can either be reflected or absorbed. You have probably heard reflected sound waves before: an echo. Harder objects are more likely to reflect sound waves. When you played the song with the cookie sheet in front of the speaker, the music was more likely to bounce back toward you. Your partner probably heard a more distorted, faint version of the song because the sound waves had trouble vibrating through the cookie sheet.

Some objects absorb sound waves. When you held the paper in front of the phone, the song was absorbed by the paper and then traveled through. Your partner was probably able to hear most of the song. The sweatshirt, however, was likely a better absorber. Your partner likely heard the song at a lower volume, maybe even muffled, depending on the thickness of the sweatshirt. In your home, carpets and curtains help to absorb sounds and slow the vibration of sound energy.

UNIT 02

FORMS OF ENERGY AND ENERGY TRANSFORMATIONS

ENERGY DOES WORK OR MAKES CHANGE. It moves planes through the air and allows you to run down the street. It bakes a cake in the oven and keeps ice frozen in the freezer. It plays our favorite songs and lights our homes. Energy makes our bodies grow and allows our minds to think. How is energy able to do so many different jobs?

Energy is classified or broken down into two categories: potential and kinetic.

FORMS OF ENERGY

POTENTIAL		KINETIC	
	Chemical Energy		Electrical Energy
	Elastic Energy		Radiant Energy
	Nuclear Energy		Thermal Energy
	Gravitational Potential Energy		Motion Energy
			Sound Energy

I. POTENTIAL ENERGY

If work is *not* being done, then there is potential energy. Ideally, the potential energy is being stored until we're ready to use it. There are four types of potential energy: chemical, nuclear, gravitational, and elastic.

2. KINETIC ENERGY

If work *is* being done, the energy used is described as kinetic, or energy in motion. There are five types of kinetic energy: radiant, mechanical, sound, thermal, and electrical.

The reason we're able to do so many things with energy is that it's constantly changing. Sometimes it changes from kinetic to potential, sometimes from potential to kinetic. It all depends on the item and its environment. These changes are called energy transformations. Energy is never really created or destroyed; it simply changes forms.

The labs in this unit will allow you to observe how energy can be transformed in common items. At the end of each lab, you'll find information on how the transformations occurred and how you might observe this transformation in the world around you.

Chemical energy turns into radiant energy in Lab 11.

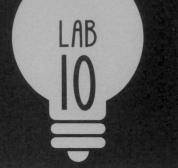

LAB 10

JUST BOUNCE

TIME:
20–30 minutes

PERSON POWER:
Grab a Crew Member! This activity is best with at least two people: one to drop the ball and one to view the rebound/bounce height.

SAFETY IS KEY:
It is helpful to remove any breakable items from your lab area during this activity. The bouncing ball could knock things over.

How does potential energy turn into kinetic energy? Is it possible to have a little bit of both? This lab explores the transformation from potential energy to kinetic energy in a bouncing super ball. How does it transfer its energy as it bounces and rebounds? You can do this indoors or out.

Fig. 2: Drop the ball while keeping the measuring tape extended.

MATERIALS

→ measuring tape
→ bouncy ball
→ kitchen counter
→ wood surface (table or deck)
→ carpet

1. Extend the measuring tape to 3' (91 cm). Stand on a foot stool, if needed. Hold the bouncy ball so that the bottom edge is at the 3' (91 cm) mark (fig. 1).

2. Have a partner watch how high the ball bounces. It can also be fun to record the bounce on video using a slow-motion feature.

3. Drop the ball with the measuring tape extended (fig. 2).

4. Have your partner record the highest point that the ball rebounds after the first bounce (fig. 3). Does it make it all the way to the top? It may be handy to make a chart like the one on the right to record your data.

5. Repeat steps 3 and 4 two more times (fig. 4). Calculate the average rebound height.

6. Choose two more heights for dropping the ball (fig. 5). Do you think a higher drop will produce a better rebound? Record your data.

7. Repeat the process on the carpet and then on a wood surface. Which surface do you think will produce the best rebound?

Fig. 1: Extend the measuring tape to 3' (91 cm).

Fig. 3: Have your partner record the highest point that the ball rebounds.

Fig. 4: Repeat for a total of three trials.

Fig. 5: Choose two more heights and drop the ball again.

	COUNTER	WOOD	CARPET
Trial 1			
Trial 2			
Trial 3			
Average			
Trial 1			
Trial 2			
Trial 3			
Average			
Trial 1			
Trial 2			
Trial 3			
Average			

ENERGY EXPLAINED

When an object is in motion, it has kinetic energy. If the object is still and in a position that gravity can act on it, it has gravitational potential energy (GPE). Your bouncy ball has GPE when you hold it at the drop height. As the ball is dropped and begins moving, its GPE is transformed into kinetic energy.

Energy is never created or destroyed, it continually changes form. When the ball hits the table, it stops for a brief moment, creates a sound, and bounces back up. In that instant, it started as kinetic energy, quickly changed to GPE, created sound energy and a little bit of thermal energy in its friction with the table, and then returned to kinetic energy as it bounced back.

Why doesn't the ball bounce back up to the point at which it was dropped? Because not all of its kinetic energy transformed into GPE—some of it was sent out as sound and thermal energy during the collision.

GLOWING BRIGHT

TIME:
15 minutes

PERSON POWER:
No Sweat!

MESS ALERT!
Use a plastic tablecloth or a newspaper under the foam cups, just in case!

SAFETY IS KEY:
Make sure the hot water is no hotter than 185°F (85°C). The glue on the glow sticks will dissolve and the glow sticks may leak in water that is too warm. If the glue breaks down, the nontoxic chemicals in the glow sticks will cause the foam cups to dissolve.

Explore the energy transformation involved in glow sticks. Is it true that they'll glow the next morning if they're kept in the freezer overnight? This lab takes a look at chemical energy, radiant energy, and thermal energy.

MATERIALS

→ **3 glow sticks of the same size and color**
→ **2 foam cups**
→ **safety glasses (optional)**
→ **hot water**
→ **cooking thermometer**
→ **ice water**
→ **kitchen tongs**

1. Examine an unbroken glow stick. What do you see inside? Notice the bubbles. Each bubble is a different chemical (fig. 1).

2. Line up the foam cups side by side and put on your safety glasses, if you have them. Carefully pour hot water into one cup to within ½" (1.3 cm) of the top. Do the same for the cold water in the second cup (fig. 2).

Fig. 4: Compare the glow sticks. What caused the difference in brightness?

3. Bend all three glow sticks until they crack. Shake them lightly to mix the chemicals.

4. Use the tongs to place one glow stick in the ice water and one in the hot water (fig. 3). Leave the third glow stick on the table. Wait for three minutes. What do you observe happening to each glow stick?

5. Take the glow sticks out of the water and compare their brightness to the glow stick that has not been in the water. What caused the difference in brightness? What energy transformation did you observe (fig. 4)?

Fig. 1. Examine the glow sticks and notice the bubbles.

Fig. 2: Pour water into the cups.

Fig. 3: Place one glow stick in the ice water and one in the hot water.

NOW TRY THIS!

What's your favorite color? Experiment with different colors of glow sticks to see if certain dyes affect the brightness. Photograph the glow sticks to help you compare. Exactly *how long* will the glow sticks last at each temperature? Try the experiment again and record how long each glow stick lasts. Add extra temperature levels if you wish. For an added twist, try taking time-lapse photographs of your glow sticks as they glow brighter or diminish in the hot and cold settings.

ENERGY EXPLAINED

Glow sticks are filled with liquid chemicals called esters, a fluorescent dye, and hydrogen peroxide. While they're separated and inactive inside the glow stick, the liquids store their potential energy as chemical energy. When you crack the glow stick, the liquids mix together and form brand new chemicals, which don't need the same amount of energy as the originals. So, they release the excess energy as radiant energy (light). A transformation occurred: chemical energy turned into radiant energy!

When you put a glow stick in cold water, it dims. The cold water absorbs some of the thermal energy (heat) from the glow stick, so the reaction slows down. When you place a glow stick in hot water, it gets brighter. The chemicals in the glow stick absorb the thermal energy from the hot water. The added energy makes the chemicals react faster and produce more light. The glow stick will glow longer in cold water than in hot water or at room temperature, because it is reacting and releasing radiant energy more slowly.

LAB 12

BUBBLING UP

TIME:
20 minutes

PERSON POWER:
No Sweat!

MESS ALERT!
Perform this activity over a plastic tablecloth or outside.

SAFETY IS KEY:
When mixing any chemicals, we recommend that you wear safety glasses. The mixture in this lab is safe to touch, but it could irritate your eyes.

Lots of things we use every day are classified as chemicals. In this lab, we'll watch energy transform as we mix two different chemicals together. Do all chemicals mix together and produce light as we saw in the previous lab? Let's find out!

Fig. 3: Measure the baking powder and add it to the bag.

📎 MATERIALS

→ **measuring spoons or medicine-sized measuring cup**
→ **resealable plastic sandwich bag**
→ **white vinegar**
→ **cooking or lab thermometer**
→ **baking soda**

1. Measure 1 teaspoon (5 ml) of vinegar and pour it into an empty plastic bag (fig. 1).

2. Feel the bag. Do you notice anything about the temperature of the vinegar?

3. Place the thermometer in the bag so that the end of it is submerged in the vinegar (fig. 2). Record the temperature.

4. Measure 1 teaspoon (5 g) of baking soda and add it to the bag (fig. 3). Gently mix it by squeezing lightly. What do you observe as the chemicals are mixing?

5. After 30 seconds take the temperature again (fig. 4). Has it changed?

6. Zip the bag closed and feel the mixture. How does it feel now compared to how it felt before?

Fig. 1: Measure the vinegar and pour it into the bag.

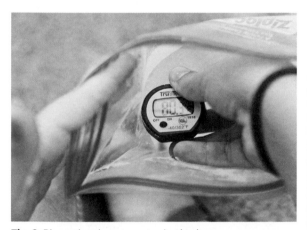

Fig. 2: Place the thermometer in the bag.

Fig. 4: After 30 seconds, take the temperature again.

ENERGY EXPLAINED

Chemical reactions take place when one chemical combines with another to form a brand new substance with different properties. Any time you mix two chemicals together to create a chemical reaction, thermal energy (heat) can be involved as the reaction takes place. Reactions can be endothermic or exothermic.

"Endo" means "in," "exo" means "out," and "thermal" means "heat." In an endothermic reaction, the thermal energy goes in—it's absorbed. An exothermic reaction is the opposite—thermal energy goes out. Which did you observe when you mixed baking soda and vinegar?

When you mixed the baking soda and vinegar, you were able to see the reaction taking place as bubbles were produced. Inside the bag, the vinegar and baking soda broke down and formed new substances: water, carbon dioxide (the bubbles), and sodium acetate. You also observed the temperature going down.

In a chemical reaction, energy is needed to break down the original materials and form the new ones. In this lab, breaking down baking soda and vinegar requires a lot of energy, so the reaction absorbs thermal energy (heat) from the surroundings, making it feel cooler. Mixing vinegar and baking soda is an endothermic reaction. The chemical energy in the chemicals is turned into thermal energy.

HOT HANDS

TIME:
20 minutes

PERSON POWER:
No Sweat!

MESS ALERT!
Perform this activity on top of a plastic tablecloth or some newspaper for easy clean up.

SAFETY IS KEY:
The hand warmer contents can become quite warm. Allow the bag to rest on the table and use caution when touching the bag. The materials are safe, but they could irritate your eyes.

In the winter, when people are standing outside at something like a sporting event, they often put hand warmers inside their gloves or in their pockets. What are these packets of warmth made of, and how do they produce thermal energy (heat)? This lab explores the energy transformation that happens in a hand warmer.

 MATERIALS

→ disposable hand warmer
→ safety glasses (optional)
→ scissors
→ resealable plastic bag
→ thermometer
→ stopwatch

1. Remove a hand warmer from the plastic wrapping. Put on your safety glasses, if using.

2. Cut open the corner of the packet. Pour the contents of the packet into an empty plastic bag and leave it unsealed (fig. 1).

3. Record the temperature quickly (fig. 2).

Fig. 2: Record the temperature quickly.

4. Allow the bag to remain open for three minutes (fig. 3).

5. Feel the bag and note the temperature. Insert the thermometer into the bag and record the temperature again. Is there a difference from earlier?

6. Seal the packet so that oxygen cannot enter the bag. Wait another three minutes.

7. After three minutes, feel and measure the temperature of the bag (fig. 4). Are there any changes to the temperature?

Fig. 1: Pour the contents of the packet into an empty plastic bag.

Fig. 3: Allow the bag to remain open for three minutes.

Fig. 4: After three minutes, feel and measure the temperature of the bag.

ENERGY EXPLAINED

One of the main ingredients in a hand-warmer packet is iron, in the form of small iron filings. The packet has tiny holes that allow oxygen and water vapor in slowly. When the iron is exposed to oxygen and water vapor in the air or on your hands, the iron reacts and begins to rust. Yes, rust! This is a chemical reaction, and it produces heat.

This chemical reaction is an exothermic reaction, because the heat is going out. Can you feel it? The chemical energy in the iron is transformed into thermal energy. It feels hot because more energy is produced by the reaction than is used to break up the iron, oxygen, and water. This extra energy is sent out as heat. When you open the packet and dump it out, the rusting process occurs much quicker than it does in the packet. This is because much more of the iron's surface is exposed to oxygen and water vapor.

BLACK AND WHITE IN THE LIGHT

Fig. 5: Check and record the temperature.

TIME:
30 minutes

PERSON POWER:
No Sweat!

MATERIALS

→ cardboard cereal box
→ scissors
→ black paper
→ white paper
→ tape
→ pencil or marker
→ 4 thermometers
→ timer

"Ugh, it's so hot today. I shouldn't have worn this dark shirt." You might hear someone say that during the summer. But why? How can wearing a dark shirt make you feel hotter on a bright, sunny day? This lab explores how energy is transformed on a sunny day and will help you decide what color shirt to wear!

1. Cut the front and back panels from the cereal box to make two equal-size pieces (fig. 1).

2. Cut the black and white paper in half (fig. 2).

3. Line up a half sheet of black paper with a half sheet of white. Tape them together, and then tape them to a box panel (fig. 3). Repeat with the other box panel.

4. Label one panel "sunny" and one panel "shady."

5. Tape a thermometer onto each color of paper on both the sunny and shady panels.

6. Record the starting temperatures of each thermometer.

7. Place one panel in the direct sunlight and one panel nearby in the shade (fig. 4).

8. Check and record the temperature of the panels every three minutes for 15 minutes (fig. 5). What do you see? Use a table like the one on the right to organize your data.

Fig. 1: Cut the front and back panels from the cereal box.

Fig. 2: Cut the black and white paper in half.

Fig. 3: Tape the black and white paper to the box panels.

Fig. 4: Place one panel in direct sunlight and one in the shade.

TIME (MIN)	TEMPERATURE OF SUNNY		TEMPERATURE OF SHADY	
	Black	White	Black	White
Starting				
3				
6				
9				
12				
15				

ENERGY EXPLAINED

"It was 100 times cooler in the shade." People say this because it *feels* hotter in the sun. When you place a panel in the sun, the sun's radiant energy, or light, is absorbed by the paper. This radiant energy is turned into thermal energy by the paper. The thermometer on the sunny piece reads the temperature of the energy absorbed by the paper *and* the air temperature around it. The shady panel is not getting additional energy from the sun; it's only measuring the thermal energy of the air around it.

You should have observed that the sunny, black page had the highest temperature. The sun produces radiant energy in all colors of the rainbow. A black object absorbs nearly all of the light that reaches it while white objects reflect most of the light. Because the black paper absorbs more energy from the sun, it gets hotter than the white sheet.

UNIT 03
RENEWABLE AND NONRENEWABLE ENERGY SOURCES

AS WE HAVE LEARNED, energy is constantly changing or transforming as work is done. We can witness this in many forms all around us. People have always used energy to do their work. Different sources of energy provide us with the ability to move our vehicles, generate electricity, heat and cool our homes, and even run down the soccer field! There are ten major energy sources, and each is classified into two groups—renewable energy sources and nonrenewable energy sources.

Supplies from renewable energy sources can be replenished in a short period of time. Renewable sources of energy include biomass, geothermal, hydropower, solar, and wind. Biomass often consists of plants, wood, garbage, and waste. Geothermal refers to the heat produced inside the core of the Earth. Hydropower is the energy that comes from flowing water, and you probably already know what solar and wind power are. These sources of energy can be used to generate electricity and create heat, but they are replenished quickly or are constantly available for our use.

Nonrenewable energy sources cannot be replenished in a short period of time. These include petroleum (oil), natural gas, coal, propane, and uranium. They can be used for energy to move cars, heat homes, generate electricity, and manufacture products, but because they cannot be replenished quickly, their supplies are limited.

These nonrenewable resources are found in the Earth in layers of rocks and minerals. They took millions to hundreds of millions of years to form. The petroleum that powers our vehicles was being formed even before dinosaurs roamed the Earth! We use lots of nonrenewable sources each year for our energy, and it's possible that we could run out of these resources in the future because they take so long to create!

The labs in this unit will allow you to explore how we find and harness each of the ten energy sources to power our lives. These activities may also allow you to get a glimpse of some of the advantages and disadvantages of each of the ten sources of energy. Each source has its benefits and drawbacks for use. Identifying and evaluating these benefits and challenges is an important part of determining how we will use energy in the future. Be on the lookout at the end of each lab for career connections and interesting energy facts!

Wind power works. →

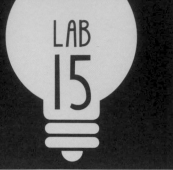

LAB 15

CANDY COLLECTOR

TIME:
30 minutes

PERSON POWER:
Grab a Crew Member!
Make sure your crew
members aren't hungry.
Candy can't be eaten
until *after* the activity is
complete!

Renewable and nonrenewable fuels power everything we do. In this lab, we'll use candies to represent each type of energy source. As the energy team for your town, you must recover the energy sources. Think carefully about how long each type will last if you continue to use energy in each round. There are two phases to the activity: past and present.

MATERIALS

→ **50 M&M's candies**
→ **2 plastic bowls**
→ **small plastic cup**
→ **2 plastic straws**
→ **timer**
→ **3 jelly beans**

1. The first phase of this lab shows how we used energy in the past. Place 50 M&M's in a bowl (fig. 1). Set the other bowl aside as the discard bowl. Place the cup near the M&M's bowl. The M&M's represent energy, and you must provide energy for your town each year. Each year will last fifteen seconds.

2. Set the timer for fifteen seconds. During that time, each person will use a straw to transfer as many M&M's into the plastic cup as possible. Use the straw for suction (fig. 2). You may *not* use your hands for anything, *not even to hold the straw!*

3. Time's up! Count how many M&M's made it into your cup. This represents the amount of energy you were able to gather and harness for this year. How much energy remains in the bowl? Place any candy in your cup into the discard bowl—this is used energy (fig. 3).

4. Repeat steps 2 and 3 for a total of four rounds (or years). Are there energy sources left for you to gather? How many more years do you think the energy will last if it's used and discarded this way?

Fig. 2: Use a straw to provide suction.

Fig. 1: Place fifty M&M's in a bowl.

Fig. 3: Place the candy from the cup into the discard bowl.

Fig. 4: Add three jelly beans to the M&M's.

Fig. 5: Return the jelly beans to the original bowl.

ENERGY EXPLAINED

The M&M's in this lab represent nonrenewable energy sources. When you collected them and transferred them to the cup, they had to be discarded. Once we access and use these sources, they are gone or discarded. The jelly beans represent renewable energy sources. These sources can be used and put back very quickly.

In the past, we didn't pay attention to how much nonrenewable energy we used. We didn't understand how long it would take for nonrenewable sources to be replenished, or how limited these sources are. By adding the use of renewable sources of energy, we can extend the life of nonrenewable sources, too. The more renewable sources we use, the longer the nonrenewables will last. Some renewable energy sources are cleaner to use, too!

5. Now let's set up the activity as if it is the present day. Place all the M&M's back in the original bowl and add three jelly beans (fig. 4). In this phase, you'll transfer candy to the cup as in step 2, but you're only required to transfer two pieces per person. Set your timer for fifteen seconds and go to it.

6. After the fifteen-second year is complete, count how many candies made it into your cup. Did you get two per team member? How many candies remain in the original bowl? Transfer all the M&M's in the cup to the discard bowl. The jelly beans can be returned to the original bowl and gathered again for future years (fig. 5)!

7. Complete three more fifteen-second years, following steps 6 and 7 for each year. Will your candies last longer now that the jellybeans are in place?

LAB 16

CHOCOLATE CHIP EXTRACTION COMPETITION

TIME:
25–30 minutes

PERSON POWER:
All Hands on Deck!

MESS ALERT!
Use a table cloth or a newspaper under your mine site.

Mining chocolate chips.

MATERIALS

→ chocolate chip cookies
→ toothpicks
→ paper clips
→ graph paper
→ pencil
→ camera phone (optional)
→ timer

1. Find a few friends to compete as separate mining companies. Or, each company can have a few team members.

Fuels, including coal and uranium, are found through mining. Today, mining must be done carefully to preserve the land and to maintain safe conditions. What is that process like? In this activity, chocolate chips represent the desired ore and the cookie represents the land in which you mine. Be careful, though! Miners must reclaim their land, or return it to its original state, when mining is complete!

2. Give each team one cookie, one toothpick, one paper clip, and one piece of graph paper.

3. Each team should place its cookie on the graph paper and trace around it with a pencil (fig. 1). If you have a camera available, take a picture.

4. Each team will use *only* the toothpick and paper clip as mining tools to extract their chocolate chip "ore." No fingers allowed (fig. 2)! Place each piece of extracted ore on an empty grid square on the graph paper outside your mining area, using only the allowed tools. Each square must contain ore to be counted.

5. Set the timer for two minutes. When time is up, count your team's squares of ore (fig. 3). Each filled square earns your company $5. Which team was the most successful?

Fig. 1: Trace your cookie on the graph paper.

Fig. 2: Use only toothpicks and paper clips as mining tools.

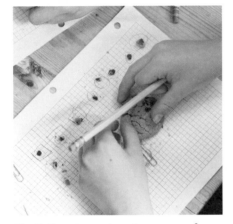

Fig. 3: Count your team's squares of ore.

Fig. 4: Reclaim your mined land by putting your cookie back together again.

6. Want to keep mining? Mine for another two minutes. Teams may choose to buy more tools for $5 each, which should be subtracted from the team's profits. Continue competing as long as teams are able to mine.

7. Refer to your cookie outline and starting photo. Reclaim your mined land by putting your cookie back together with the materials remaining in the traced area (fig. 4). Try to make your cookie look like it did when you started.

8. Talk with the other teams. What makes a successful mining company? If you have to put the land back together after you are finished mining, does it always make sense to try and get every chip? What if you also have to buy your land and pay your miners? How difficult might it be to make money on your mine?

ENERGY EXPLAINED

Reclamation is the process of returning the land that was used by an industry to its original state—or better. This means if a company removed a forest to mine land, they must reforest the land with the same type of trees that once grew there and monitor their growth. If there was a species of bird that lived there, a habitat must be created to allow those birds to return.

Reclamation helps prevent erosion, restore biological balance in the mined area, and account for safe land use. Companies are required by law to complete the process and must set aside money to guarantee that reclamation will occur at the end of the mining.

Companies often work with local municipalities or state governments to ensure the condition of the land meets local approval.

LAB 17

GETTING THE OIL OUT

TIME:
15–20 minutes

PERSON POWER:
Grab a Crew Member!

MESS ALERT!
Set up this activity inside and complete the activity outdoors or on the kitchen floor, in case spills occur.

SAFETY IS KEY:
When it's time to get the oil out, you may need to stand on a stool or chair. Make sure you have a friend or adult spotting you.

→
Fig. 4: Stand on a stool so that the well casing forms a straight line from your mouth to the cola.

Petroleum, or crude oil, is found thousands of feet below the Earth's surface. In order to bring oil to the surface, companies must drill down several thousand feet, creating a well. Many sections of pipe, called well casing, are put in, giving the oil an easy pathway to the surface. If the oil does not seep up on its own, machines can create artificial pressure to suck the liquids to the surface. How much pressure needs to be applied? Let's drill for oil to simulate this process!

MATERIALS

→ scissors
→ 8 plastic drinking straws
→ masking tape
→ cola
→ 3-oz (88 ml) plastic cups
→ chocolate syrup
→ ruler

1. Using the scissors, cut a ⅓" (1 cm) slit at one end of each straw (fig. 1).

2. Join the straws end to end, forming one long tube, by placing the slit end of one straw inside the next (fig. 2).

3. Place masking tape over each connection to secure the straw joints and create an air-tight seal (fig. 3).

4. Pour some cola into a plastic cup. This will represent the oil. Place your oil well on the floor.

Fig. 1: Cut a slit at one end of each straw.

Fig. 2: Join the straws end to end to form one long tube.

Fig. 3: Place masking tape over each connection.

Fig. 5: Pour chocolate syrup into a cup and try to bring it to the surface through the straws.

ENERGY EXPLAINED

Viscosity is a property of liquids. It describes how much the liquid resists flowing. High-viscosity liquids are thick and slow moving. Low-viscosity liquids are the opposite: thin and runny.

Crude oil from the ground comes in many viscosities and colors, depending on its location and how it was formed. Some crude oil is dark brown and viscous (thick), almost like molasses or chocolate syrup. Other crude oil can be a clear, yellowish color with very low viscosity.

5. Place one end of your straw tubing into the cola so that it sticks straight into the air. This will represent your oil well casing.

6. If necessary, stand on a stool so that the well casing forms a straight line from your mouth to the cola (fig. 4). Now suck on the end of the straw to try to bring the liquid to the top of the well casing.

7. If it's difficult, perhaps air is getting in through the casing's seams. Wrap additional tape around the joints in the casing. Can you get the oil out of the well now?

8. Try a few variations. Pour some chocolate syrup into a cup. Replace the cup of cola with the cup of syrup. Try to bring the chocolate syrup to the surface using the same technique (fig. 5). Is it harder?

9. Decrease the length of the casing by cutting off one straw. What do you notice when you try to bring liquids to the surface now?

NOW TRY THIS!

Continue to experiment with different viscosities of liquids and different configurations of straws. Try to find the best well casing set-up for each viscosity.

LAB 18

PERFORATED PERFECTION

TIME:
20 minutes

PERSON POWER:
Grab a Crew Member!

MESS ALERT!
Perform this Lab outdoors or on a plastic tablecloth. Things might get a little slippery!

Fig. 3: Slowly pour water on the sponges.

If you imagine drilling for oil is like sucking through a drinking straw, how many openings would you need to bring the fluids up to the straw's surface? Well, just one. This lab will explore a few techniques employed by drilling companies to allow more fluids to flow into a well. Do more holes mean more fluids? Let's test it out!

Fig. 1: Place a sponge on the plastic wrap and lay one of the straws on top.

Fig. 2: Lay the second sponge on top so that all the edges line up.

MATERIALS

→ 2 foam plates or meat trays (clean)
→ plastic wrap
→ 2 kitchen sponges, (dry or barely moist) of the same size and shape
→ flexible drinking straws
→ masking tape
→ water in a liquid measuring cup
→ 3 identical books or weights
→ 1 oz (30 ml) graduated cylinder or medicine measuring cup
→ push pin
→ ruler
→ paper towels

1. Lay out one of the foam trays. Cut a large piece of plastic wrap and lay it across the tray.

2. Place one sponge on top of the plastic wrap and tray. Lay one of the straws on top of the sponge so that the bottom edge of the straw is inside the edges of the sponge and the elbow end hangs off the other end (fig. 1).

3. Lay the other sponge on top of the straw/sponge set-up, so that all the sponge edges match up (fig. 2).

4. Slowly pour water on the sponges so that they become saturated, but little or no water is leaking out (fig. 3). Keep track of how much water you used.

5. Cover the sponges and straw with plastic wrap (fig. 4). Try to create a sealed package with no places for water to escape. Use tape to help seal it.

6. Place the second foam dish under the exposed end of the straw. This tray will collect fluids.

7. Lay books, one at a time, on top of the sponges and observe the amount of water that comes out of the straw and onto the collection tray (fig. 5).

Fig. 4: Cover the sponges and straw with plastic wrap.

Press by hand if additional pressure is required or if the books are so heavy that they kink or crush the straw. Continue until no more water exits the straw.

8. Measure the amount of water in the collection dish by pouring it into the graduated cylinder (fig. 6).

9. Disassemble the stack of sponges. Drain or squeeze out the sponges to remove any remaining water.

10. Using a push pin, poke several holes about ⅛" (3 mm) apart at the long end of the straw, farthest from the elbow (fig. 7). If your straw is striped, use the stripes as the guide for hole punching!

11. Lay out a new piece of plastic wrap with a sponge on top. Place the straw from step 10 on this sponge, and place the other sponge on top, as in step 3. Repeat steps 4 to 8, using the same amount of water to saturate the sponges. Do you notice a difference in the amount of water collected?

Fig. 5: Lay books on top of the sponges.

Fig. 6: Measure the amount of water in the collection dish.

Fig. 7: Use a pin to poke holes in the long end of the straw.

ENERGY EXPLAINED

This lab demonstrates several important things that occur when drilling for oil and natural gas. In the first part of the activity, the straw has only one opening for fluids to enter the well casing and be brought to the surface. In the second part, after perforating the straw (your well casing), you should have noticed an increase in the amount of liquid produced from the sponges (your well). Well cases are perforated during the drilling process using an explosive charge. They allow for oil and natural gas to flow into the well casing from all directions, not just one opening.

You may be wondering why the activity in this lab was done horizontally. Oil wells are drilled vertically, but special robotic or directional drilling techniques are also used to drill horizontally from the same well. This allows oil and gas to flow from many directions into the well. It also means that we can drill one well that draws further from the original location, rather than drilling at several different spots at the surface! Oh, and those sponges? Yeah, they've got pores that trapped the water in the sponge, much like the way sedimentary rocks trap oil and natural gas!

PROPANE is not a pain to find!

Propane is on the list of the ten energy sources. But how do we find it in the world around us? Propane is a product that can be separated from oil and natural gas. When we have oil or natural gas, we often have propane, too! Propane is very useful; it can be used for fueling grills, heating farm buildings, drying crops, generating electricity, and even powering forklifts and other vehicles.

LAB 19

FRACTURING GELATIN

TIME:
30 minutes, plus
one overnight
for gelatin to set

PERSON POWER:
All Hands on Deck! This
activity requires a few
hands. Have an adult
help with preparing the
gelatin. It might be fun to
have a friend record your
fracturing on video!

MESS ALERT!
This activity is best
completed on a plastic
tablecloth or on
newspaper. Keep paper
towels and warm water
on standby for cleaning
up sticky situations.

SAFETY IS KEY:
Boiling water is needed
for preparing gelatin.
Ask an adult for help
with this step!

Natural gas is a fossil fuel much
like petroleum. The two have very
similar properties because they
were formed under the same
conditions, but natural gas is, of
course, a gas, and petroleum is a
liquid. North America has a large
supply of natural gas, which is
a nonrenewable fuel. Bubbles of
natural gas are often trapped
in tiny little pores of rocks—just
as the pores in your face trap
oil, dirt, and air! In order to open
these pores and release the
natural gas, companies sometimes use a technique called
hydraulic fracturing. This lab
explores how fractures are
created underground.

 MATERIALS

→ water
→ saucepan or teapot
→ large measuring cup
→ 3 packets of unflavored gelatin
→ wire whisk
→ loaf pan
→ nonstick cooking spray
→ spatula

Fig. 5: Push on the syringe's plunger and inject the syrup
into the gelatin block.

→ dinner plate
→ flexible drinking straws
→ ruler (with metric measurements)
→ push pin
→ plastic wrap
→ plastic oral syringe for medicine
 (1½ tablespoons/22 ml)
→ tape
→ pancake syrup
→ plastic knife
→ paper towels

Fig. 1: Insert a straw into the side of the gelatin.

1. Prepare the gelatin the night before you plan to complete this lab. Gelatin can be kept in the refrigerator until it's time for fracturing fun! Follow these steps to prepare the gelatin:

    a. Boil water on the stove in a saucepan or teakettle.

    b. While the water is boiling, fill the large measuring cup with ½ cup (118 ml) of room-temperature water.

    c. Sprinkle three packets of gelatin over the room temperature water and mix it using the whisk.

    d. Add 3½ cups (828 ml) of boiling water. You should now have 4 cups (946 ml) of liquid. Whisk to continue dissolving the gelatin.

    e. Spray the inside of the loaf pan with cooking spray and pour the gelatin solution into the pan.

    f. Refrigerate overnight.

2. Cut the gelatin into four or five blocks with the plastic knife. Using the spatula, remove one block and place it on the dinner plate.

3. Insert a straw in the side of the gelatin block so that the straw is parallel to the plate (fig. 1). Insert it about half to two-thirds of the way into the block, being careful not to allow it to exit the opposite side.

4. To bore out the hole you've created, twist the straw and slowly remove it from gelatin, bringing the excess gelatin with it. Discard this straw.

ENERGY EXPLAINED

Hydraulic fracturing is used to help oil companies gain access to natural gas (and oil) that is trapped in the tiny pores of rocks thousands of feet below the Earth's surface.

Technicians drill down, creating an opening cased with metal pipe. They then pump a fluid into the well at high pressure. This fluid is usually made mostly of water, something slippery (like soap), and a little sand. When the fluid strikes the rocks at high pressure, like your syrup did, it has nowhere to go, so it causes the rocks to crack slightly around the well bore. You saw this happen with the fractures that appeared in the gelatin around the hole that you bored with a straw. These cracks, or fractures, allow the tiny pores in the rock to open up so that oil and natural gas can escape and be pulled to the surface. At the surface, oil and natural gas will be separated from the injected fluids and processed for use in cooking, powering factories, and generating electricity.

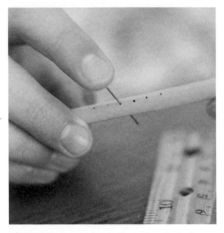

Fig. 2: Use a push pin to poke six holes through both sides of the straw.

Fig. 4: Fill the syringe with syrup.

Fig. 3: Cover the end of the straw with plastic wrap.

5. Lay a fresh straw along the ruler's metric edge. Beginning about 10 mm in from the long end of the straw, use the push pin to poke six holes into the straw, making each hole 3 to 5 mm apart (fig. 2). If the push pin doesn't go through both sides, rotate the straw and make six more holes directly across from the first set.

6. Cover this end of the straw with a small piece of plastic wrap to prevent any leaking through the holes during the next few steps (fig. 3).

7. Attach the other end of the straw to the syringe using tape and/or plastic wrap for a good seal.

8. Remove the plunger from the syringe and fill the syringe with syrup from the large opening at the top (fig. 4). It's easiest to hold the syringe at an angle while you do this. You want the syrup to begin running down into the straw. Continue until most of the straw and syringe are full.

Fig. 6: Observe what you see happening and notice the fractures.

9. Quickly replace the plunger in the top of the syringe to keep the syrup from gushing out. It may still drip a bit.

10. Remove the plastic wrap from the pin holes at the other the end of the straw. Insert this end of the straw into the hole you bored in the gelatin block.

11. Using very firm pressure, *quickly* push on the syringe's plunger and inject the syrup into the gelatin block (fig. 5).

12. Observe what happens to the gelatin and take note of any fractures you might see (fig. 6). Pull the straw out and begin the clean-up process, or repeat with another gelatin block!

POROSITY

Have you ever heard something described as porous? An object is porous if it has holes or openings that can trap liquids or gases. Your face, sponges, strawberry shortcake, and even some rocks can be porous.

Rocks that were formed over hundreds of millions of years by sand and dirt piling on top of more sand and dirt and sediment are called sedimentary rocks. As they formed, little pockets of air remained between the pieces of dirt and sediment. Some rocks have smaller pockets, and some have larger or different-shaped pockets, depending on what the conditions were like as they were formed. These pockets are called pores. Rocks that have lots of pores are said to have a high porosity.

Sometimes fossil material—like plants or tiny sea animals (plankton)—was also trapped in the rocks. As the fossil matter decayed and pressure was added, oil and natural gas were created and trapped in the pores. The oil and gas can flow from pore to pore if the pores are very close together. Some pores, however, are not close together and don't allow for this to happen. Geologists look for natural gas and oil in rocks that have a high porosity. The pores don't have to be big, they just have to have a lot of pockets to trap the good stuff!

LAB 20

URANIUM MILLER

TIME:
45 minutes

PERSON POWER:
No Sweat! This activity can be completed easily on your own, but for safety purposes it may be helpful to grab a crew member, and maybe even an adult crew member!

MESS ALERT!
This activity should be completed on top of a tablecloth or newspaper. It could get a bit messy!

SAFETY IS KEY:
You have the option of using a stove or burner to complete this lab. Use caution handling pots and glassware that are hot. Check with an adult before using the stove or burner.

Uranium is the fuel used in nuclear power plants to generate electricity. It's an element found most commonly in ores and rock, but in order to use the uranium, we have to separate it from the ore. This process is called milling. You will become the miller in this lab as you attempt to separate salt, sand, and gravel in a mixture, and capture only the salt—much as is done in the uranium milling process. We've used grams in this lab because the measurements are so small. One gram = 0.03 ounces!

MATERIALS

→ digital kitchen scale
→ 10 grams sand
→ 10 grams salt
→ 5 grams gravel or rocks
→ plastic cup or bowl
→ small piece of screen or wire mesh
→ water
→ coffee filter
→ beaker or glass measuring cup
→ measuring spoons
→ small cooking pot
→ metal spoon

1. Mix the sand, salt, and gravel in a plastic cup or bowl. Make sure it is well mixed. If you don't use the measurements listed, be sure to note how much of each item you use. For this activity, salt will represent the uranium, while sand and gravel will be the waste ore.

Fig. 1: Pour the sand, salt, and gravel mixture through the screen.

2. Begin trying to mill for uranium by pouring the mixture through the screen (fig. 1). Remove the largest particles and set them aside.

Fig. 2: Pour the water/ore mixture over the filter.

Fig. 3: Pour the remaining mixture into the pot.

Fig. 4: Collect any solid material that remains in the pot.

3. Mix the remaining ore with 3 to 5 tablespoons (44 to 74 ml) of water. Stir well.

4. Put a coffee filter over the glass beaker or measuring cup. Slowly pour the water/ore mixture over the filter (fig. 2). The material that collects on the filter is waste ore. Remove the filter and waste ore and set them aside.

5. Pour the remaining water mixture into the pot (fig. 3). Boil the solution until all of the water evaporates.

6. Collect any solid material or residue that remains in the pot or on the sides of the pot (fig. 4). This is the uranium. How much uranium remains? Place it on the kitchen scale to see if the weight is similar to the weight you started with.

NOW TRY THIS!

For a quick math application, calculate the percentage of mined material you recovered from milling. You started with 25 total grams of material. Take the mass of the uranium (salt) at the end and divide by 25 grams to find your percentage of uranium recovered. What percentage was waste rock?

ENERGY EXPLAINED

Rocks are mixtures of materials that can be separated. When we separate materials in certain rocks and ores, we find useful things like gold, tin, aluminum, and uranium!

When uranium ore is mined, it is brought to a mill where it is ground into fine particles, just as you started with in this lab. In the milling process, chemicals are often added to dissolve the uranium and separate it from the waste ore—just like you dissolved the salt in the water!

Every uranium mine contains a different amount of uranium. The milling process can recover tiny amounts of uranium or very large amounts depending on the ore. Once the uranium is separated out, it's dried and processed into pellets the size of a pencil eraser. These pellets are used at nuclear power plants to generate electricity through a process called nuclear fission.

LAB 21

WIND DOES WORK

Fig. 6: Blow air toward your pinwheel to test it.

TIME:
30 minutes

PERSON POWER:
No Sweat! or
Grab a Crew Member!

For centuries, we've been harnessing wind to do work. Moving air can be used to pump water, grind grain, move boats, and generate electricity. Wind turbines that generate electricity work in the same way as a windmill that might grind grain or pump water. Build a windmill and explore just how much work moving air can do. Invite some friends and hold a windmill competition!

MATERIALS

→ pencil
→ printer paper or construction paper
→ scissors
→ hole punch
→ foam cup
→ plastic straw
→ marker
→ ruler
→ masking tape
→ plastic stirrer straw
→ straight pins
→ string
→ paper clips
→ small binder clip
→ electric fan

1. Trace with a pencil or photocopy the windmill-blade template on page 71 onto a piece of paper.

2. Cut out the square outline. Cut along the dotted diagonal lines.

3. Punch holes in the four corner black dots and the center dot (fig. 1).

4. Turn the foam cup upside-down on your work surface.

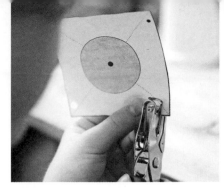

Fig. 1: Punch holes in the corners and center of the template.

Fig. 2: Cut and tape a piece of straw to the bottom of the cup.

Fig. 3: Make an axle from the stirrer straw. Insert a straight pin through the stirrer.

5. Place the straw on top of the bottom of the cup. With a marker and ruler, measure a piece of straw slightly longer than the diameter of the bottom of the cup. Tape the piece across the bottom of the cup (fig. 2). This will hold the windmill's central axle.

6. Make the central axle for the windmill blade from the stirrer straw. Be sure the stirrer is at least 2" (5 cm) longer than the diameter of the bottom of the cup. Mark a spot ⅜" (1 cm) from the end of the stirrer. Insert a straight pin through the stirrer at this spot so the pin head is up against the stirrer (fig. 3). This short end of the stirrer will be the front of the axle.

7. Insert the front of the axle through the center hole of the windmill template. Let the paper rest against the pin. Slip each corner of the template over the end of the axle so that all the holes overlap and four windmill blades are formed (fig. 4). Be careful not to crease the blades. Secure the blades by inserting another straight pin into the axle. Use tape to secure the blades if the pin is too loose.

8. Insert the long end of the axle into the straw on top of the cup.

9. Cut a 16" (41 cm) length of string. Tape the end of the string to the back end of the axle (fig. 5). Tie the other end of the string to a paper clip. Make sure there is at least 12" (30 cm) of string between the axle and the top of the paper clip.

ENERGY EXPLAINED

Wind *can* do work! In this lab, you were able to build a functional windmill. Over history, windmills have been used to pump water, hoist heavy items, crush grains and rocks, and even run printing presses! In 1888, a farmer realized that he could generate electricity to power devices in his home with the moving parts of a windmill. His first wind turbine had 144 blades that turned belts, pulleys, and a generator built by the farmer. This model looked very similar in shape to the model you built, and it was able to power over 350 lights—pretty good for the first turbine.

Modern wind turbines come in all shapes and sizes and can be found in fields, on mountaintops, and even at museums and sports stadiums. They often consist of three blades, rather than the four in your windmill. Today's large turbines can power up to 1,000 homes!

Fig. 4: Slip each corner of the template over the end of the axle to form four windmill blades.

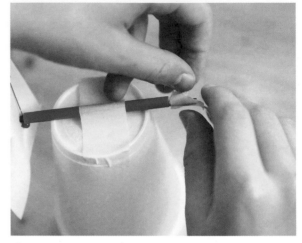

Fig. 5: Tape the end of the string to the back end of the axle.

10. Fasten a small binder clip to the back end of the axle for balance and to keep the string from sliding off.

11. Slide the axle forward so that the binder clip touches the end of the straw. Insert another straight pin through the axle at the front end so that the blades spin without hitting the cup. Blow air toward your pinwheel to test this and adjust as necessary (fig. 6).

12. Place the windmill in front of the fan. Watch the blades spin, wind the string, and lift the paper clip to the top (fig. 7). Continue adding paper clips to see how many your windmill can lift.

NOW TRY THIS!

Redesign your model to do more work. How could it be used to lift more paper clips, lift heavier items, or even do a *different* type of work?

Fig. 7: Place the windmill in front of the fan so that the blades spin.

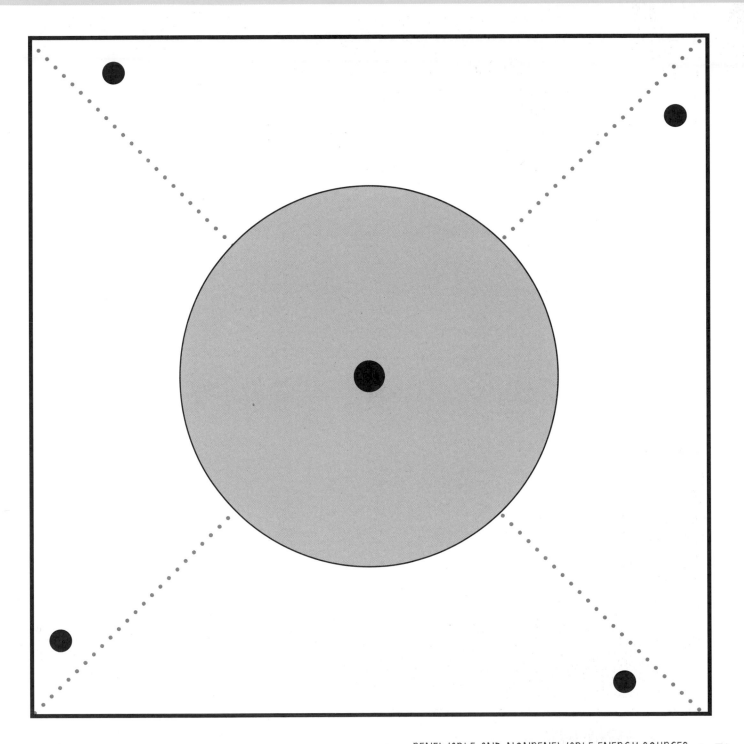

LAB 22

GEOTHERMAL HEATER

TIME:
45 minutes

PERSON POWER:
No Sweat! However, it might be fun to grab a crew member for less mess.

MESS ALERT!
This activity should be done on a kitchen counter or table covered with a plastic tablecloth. There will be drips, so have towels or paper towels handy!

SAFETY IS KEY:
This lab requires hot water. Use caution, because splashes and drips can burn, and water that is too hot could melt the cups and straws! Use caution when pouring water as it may be near a heating pad used in the lab. Water and electrical devices should not come in contact.

Fig. 4: Tape the V-shaped straws to the inside bottom of the baking dish, and position the cups outside the dish.

Geothermal means heat from within the Earth. The Earth's core is very hot. This heat radiates up through the layers of rock between us and the core. In some places, there is enough heat to create magma in a volcano and geysers that erupt with steamy water! Geothermal energy at very high temperatures can also generate electricity.

Not every area is exposed to geothermal energy hot spots, but we can still use the constant temperature below the surface to heat or cool our homes and water. This lab will show you how geothermal energy can be used to exchange or pump fluid out of your home and replace it with fluid at a warmer or cooler temperature—from just below the Earth's surface!

Fig. 1: Poke a hole in the bottom of a cup. This will be your drain cup.

Fig. 2: Select three straws. Fit them together end to end and tape over the joints.

📎 MATERIALS

→ **2 small plastic cups**
→ **nail**
→ **scissors**
→ **4 flexible straws**
→ **tape**
→ **tongs**
→ **13" x 9" (33 x 23 cm) baking dish**
→ **heating pad**
→ **paper towels**
→ **dish towel**
→ **digital thermometer**
→ **ice**
→ **cold water**
→ **notebook and pencil**
→ **oven mitt**
→ **hot water**

1. Poke a hole in the bottom of one cup using the nail or scissors. This will be your drain cup (fig. 1). Poke a hole in the second cup ½" to 1" (1.3 to 2.5 cm) from the top. This will be your collection cup.

2. Select three straws. Note that the section of the straws below the elbow is longer than the section above. Use the scissors to cut small slits into the long end of three straws. Pinch the sliced end of one straw and insert it into the short, unsliced end of the second straw. Tape over the joint. Repeat this so that all three cut straws are connected. Connect the last edge to the remaining straw (fig. 2).

3. Insert the first straw's short end through the hole you created in the collection cup (fig. 3). Trim this end of the straw if it hits the other side of the cup due to the diameter of the cup and length of the elbow. You want the elbow be inserted far enough into the cup so that water drips in but does not leak back out. Use tape to secure the straw around the opening, if needed.

4. Insert the opposite end of the connected straws into the drain cup through the bottom hole. Use tongs to pull the straw up through, and use tape to secure it around the opening, if needed.

5. Bend the elbow of the straw below the drain cup. Bend the next elbow in the straw line as well. Lay these flat so they make a V-shape and the drain cup is upright. Tape the V-shaped straws inside the bottom of the baking dish and position the cups outside the baking dish, next to the two corners of one long side of the dish (fig. 4). The drain cup will be slightly elevated off the table; the collection cup should rest on the table. Tape the straws to the dish so the cups and straws remain in position.

6. Turn on the heating pad to the highest setting. Center the baking dish on top of the heating pad. NOTE: Make sure no part of the heating pad is under the cups, in case a drip occurs. Arrange paper towels under the cups so that drips are absorbed by the paper towels and *not* the heating pad.

7. Place a dish towel over the straws inside the dish. Wait ten minutes for the heating to occur.

8. Pour ice water into the drain cup. Measure the temperature with the thermometer (fig. 5). Record the temperature.

9. Water should begin to fill the collection cup. Take the temperature of this water (fig. 6). Has the temperature changed? Remove the cups from the straws and drain any water in the cups and straws. Turn off the heating pad and remove it from the area.

Fig. 3: Insert the first straw's short end through the hole you made in the collection cup in step 1.

10. Try to reverse the conditions! Heat some water to no more than 100°F (38°C). Do not use water at a higher temperature.

11. Make sure the V-shaped straws are secured to the dish and the straws are inserted back into the cups and sealed with tape. Fill the baking dish with ice. Cover the dish with the dish towel.

12. Pour hot water into the drain cup and take the temperature at the start. Record the temperature in your notebook.

13. Take the temperature of the water that fills the collection cup. Do you notice a difference in temperature from the drain cup?

Fig. 5: Pour ice water into the drain cup. Measure the temperature.

Fig. 6: Take the temperature of the water in the collection cup.

ENERGY EXPLAINED

Geothermal energy from the Earth can heat and cool other substances through conduction. In high-temperature geothermal plants, a geothermal vent heats a pool of water to create steam. The steam is used to generate electricity. Some places on the globe, such as Iceland, and parts of California, are geothermal hotspots, where creating this steam is natural! But even in places where heat from the Earth's core isn't as evident, you'd find that the ground remains a fairly constant temperature just four to six feet below the surface thanks to geothermal energy!

On the surface, the ground temperature changes with the weather each day. In winter or in cold climates, we can use a heat exchanger in our homes to pump up air or water from a few feet below the surface. This fluid will be warmer than water or air at the surface, and, through conduction, it exchanges heat, making our home systems do a little less work heating air and water! This is what you observed in the first part of the activity. By pumping the cold water toward a warmer area, the water exits the system a bit warmer in the collection cup.

In summer or in warm climates, the air at the surface is probably warmer than the air just below the surface. Heat exchangers can work to keep homes cool, too. By running the warm fluids near cooler fluid from below the surface, the warm fluid is cooled, too! This is just like the second part of the activity—so hot, but so cool!

SOLAR COOKER

TIME:
1 hour or more (set-up and cooking)

PERSON POWER:
Grab a Crew Member! Cooking is always more fun with a friend. You can even do this as a challenge to see who has built the best oven.

SAFETY IS KEY:
Consider the foods you wish to cook in your oven. Be sure to cook items that will not make you sick if they're undercooked. Use the oven thermometer to make sure your food has been adequately warmed.

Ever hear the phrase, "It was so hot outside, you could fry an egg"? This can actually work! The sun's radiant energy travels to Earth as light. If you can trap this light as heat, the oven effect takes place. If you've ever left a candy bar in the car on a hot day, you know what we mean. In this lab, we'll set up our own solar cooker for use on a sunny day.

MATERIALS

→ **small cardboard pizza box**
→ **marker**
→ **ruler**
→ **scissors**
→ **aluminum foil**
→ **plastic wrap**
→ **masking tape**
→ **black construction paper**
→ **paper plate**
   (dark colors work best)
→ **wooden skewer**
→ **oven thermometer (optional)**
→ **food to cook (such as cookie dough, nacho chips and shredded cheese, or carrots)**

Fig. 5: Take your solar cooker outside.

1. On the top of the pizza box, use the marker to draw a square with edges 1" (2.5 cm) from all sides of the box.

2. Use the scissors to cut along the marked lines on the side and front edges, but leave the hinge edge uncut (fig. 1).

3. Tape aluminum foil to the inside surface of this flap (fig. 2). Make sure the shiny side of the foil is facing out. This will reflect sunlight into the box. Smooth out any wrinkles that might occur.

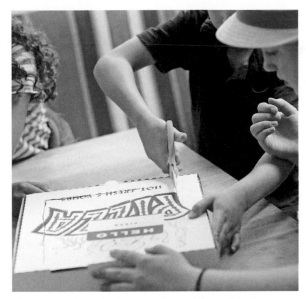

Fig. 1: Cut along the lines on three sides of the box top, leaving the fourth as a hinge.

Fig. 2: Tape foil to the inside surface of the flap.

ENERGY EXPLAINED

The sun's radiant energy travels to Earth and strikes your oven as light. The shiny, foil-coated flap helps to bounce some extra energy onto your food from several angles. The light travels through the transparent plastic wrap and is absorbed by the food inside and the black paper coating on the bottom. The food and the black paper transform the light into heat, or thermal energy.

As your oven sits in the sunlight, more and more light is transformed into heat. But this heat cannot travel back through the plastic wrap—it's trapped! The thermal energy builds and more energy is absorbed by the food inside, allowing it to cook. It's easy to understand how this activity will work on a summer day, but you can cook food on a sunny winter's day, too. It might take a bit longer, but light transforms to thermal energy just the same way!

NOW TRY THiS!

Add insulation to your oven. Use some newspaper, bubble wrap, or cotton balls around the inside perimeter of your box. These materials will take up the empty space in the box and trap more heat inside the oven! Does it cook your food more quickly?

Fig. 3: Tape plastic wrap over the rest of the box lid.

Fig. 4: Tape black construction paper inside the bottom of the box.

4. With the reflector flap lifted, tape plastic wrap over the rest of the box lid (fig. 3). The plastic wrap will cover the flap hole you just made. Seal the edges with tape.

5. Open the box lid completely. Tape more plastic wrap to the underside of the lid's flap hole, and seal any air leaks with tape.

6. Tape black construction paper inside the bottom of the box (fig. 4).

7. Prepare your food on a paper plate. Dark paper plates can be helpful to absorb extra light. Take the paper plate of food, the skewer, tape, thermometer, and box outside (fig. 5).

Fig. 6: Find a flat, level surface to do your cooking.

Fig. 7: Keep the reflector flap tilted back to collect light.

8. Find a flat, level surface in the sunlight to do your cooking (fig. 6). Place the food items inside the oven with the thermometer and close the box lid, keeping the reflector flap tilted back to collect light (fig. 7). Tape the wooden skewer to the reflector lid and use it to prop the flap up. Make sure your oven is facing the sun so that sunlight strikes the reflector flap and shines onto your food.

9. Allow your oven to heat up, cooking your food. Depending on the type of food you're cooking and where you live, your food could be warmed in minutes or maybe hours. Check your food every five to ten minutes. Make sure to adjust your oven position and reflector flap position as the sun's angle changes. Is it done (fig. 8)? Enjoy!

Fig. 8: Enjoy!

BIOMASS BAG

Fig. 1: Take the bag inside and add some food scraps.

TIME:
15 minutes, plus a few minutes each day for 1 to 2 weeks

PERSON POWER:
No Sweat!

MATERIALS

→ **resealable plastic bag**
→ **yard waste (leaves, grass clippings, etc.)**
→ **leftover food scraps (lettuce, pizza crust, etc.)**
→ **packet of powdered yeast**
→ **water**
→ **camera or camera phone**
→ **notebook and pencil**

Biomass energy is energy that comes from living things. Wood, garbage, animal waste, landfill gas, and crops all count as biomass. None of these items can give off their energy until they are burned, fermented, or decayed. In this lab, we'll make some biomass in a bag!

1. Open the plastic bag. Grab some yard waste items that you find outdoors, or pick some leaves, flowers, and grass and put them in your bag.

2. Take the bag inside and add some food scraps. It's best to avoid meat, but veggies, fruit, or even some old pizza crust will do! Make sure your bag has empty space, too (fig. 1).

3. Add a pinch of yeast to the collection in the bag (fig. 2).

4. Add a few drops of water so that the mixture is moist.

5. Force as much air as possible out of the bag before sealing it (fig. 3). Take a picture of the bag and note anything you see on day 1.

6. Place the bag in a warm place, like a windowsill, and allow it to stay there for a week or more (fig. 4). Snap a picture each day and compare what you see happening to the contents of the bag and the space in the bag.

Fig. 2: Add a pinch of yeast to the bag.

Fig. 3: Force as much air out of the bag as possible.

Fig. 4: Place the bag in a warm place, like a windowsill.

French Fry Fuel

Biodiesel and ethanol are fuels that are created from biomass. Ethanol is made by fermenting corn, grass, or sugarcane, which creates a liquid that can power our vehicles. Ethanol is put into gasoline in the U.S. in small percentages, and some cars use as much as 85 percent ethanol. It's even used in race cars! Biodiesel is a diesel fuel that is made from plant oils or animal fats and grease. Biodiesel is added to diesel fuel just like ethanol, or it can be used by itself in cars and pickup trucks and even garbage trucks and buses. People can make their own biodiesel easily by collecting fryer oil and grease from restaurants that make fried food!

ENERGY EXPLAINED

Since biomass comes from something that was once living, these items originally got their energy from the sun. Plants grew because of photosynthesis, during which they made food from light. We often burn these plants and wood to release the energy stored during this process.

Biomass decays over time. While doing so, we can often smell something that signals decay. We can trap the gases given off during the decay process and burn them for energy, too! This is how landfills make energy—they trap the rotting garbage gas and burn it!

This decay process was occurring in your plastic bag. When you added yeast to organic material, it created a process called fermentation, where the yeast, a fungus, helps to break down the biomass and convert it into alcohol and gas. This process, on a much larger scale, is how ethanol fuel is made.

Did you notice the materials in the bag change and the bag start to expand? You were observing fermentation and decay! Heat helps these decaying and fermenting processes occur; that's why we placed it in a warm spot.

DAM FUN

Fig. 5: Line up the bottle in the pan so the holes face outward.

TIME:
20 minutes

PERSON POWER:
Grab a Crew Member!

MESS ALERT!
This activity should be done outside or on a kitchen counter, as things can get a bit slippery!

Hydropower is energy that comes from the force of moving water. Usually, we harness this energy in rivers. A dam is built to control the water and create a reservoir that is able to focus the flow of water toward a turbine that is attached to a generator. Does it make a difference how high the water is in the reservoir? This lab will allow you to explore how height and force are related at a hydropower dam.

MATERIALS

→ **2-liter soda bottle with cap and smooth sides**
→ **wallpaper pan**
→ **marker**
→ **push pin**
→ **water**
→ **duct tape**
→ **paper towels**
→ **notebook and pencil**

1. Remove the sticker or label from the outside of the soda bottle and make sure it is dry.

2. Place the ruler in the wallpaper pan and make marks on the bottom of the pan every inch (2.5 cm) until you reach the end of the pan (fig. 1).

3. Place the bottle in the wallpaper pan. Use the ruler to measure up from the bottom of the bottle. Mark the bottle at 2", 4", 6", and 8" (5 cm, 10 cm, 15 cm, and 20 cm) (fig. 2).

4. Use the push pin to make holes at each of the marks in the bottle (fig. 3). Cover each hole with a piece of duct tape (fig. 4).

5. Fill the bottle with water to the 8" (20 cm) line. Seal the cap to prevent any leaking around the taped lines.

Fig. 1: Mark the bottom of the pan every inch (2.5 cm).

Fig. 2: Mark the bottle at 2" (5 cm) intervals.

Fig. 3: Make a hole at each of the marks with a push pin.

Fig. 4: Cover each hole with duct tape.

6. Line up the bottle in the wallpaper pan so the holes are facing outward toward the lines in the pan (fig. 5). Remove the duct tape from the 2" (5 cm) mark. How far does the water shoot? Record the distance in your notebook.

7. Close the cap, seal the hole with tape, and uncap and refill the bottle to the 8" (20 cm) line. Place the bottle back in the pan.

8. Repeat steps 6 and 7 for a total of three trials.

9. Dry the outside of the bottle and tape the hole closed. Follow steps 5 through 8 at the other three marks, repeating each one for three trials. Which height caused the water to push out with the greatest force?

ENERGY EXPLAINED

Hydropower facilities usually have a dam to hold back the water. If you've ever seen a dam, you probably noticed that the water typically falls at a dam. This effect is important, as you witnessed in this lab. At a dam, the water is channeled from the reservoir toward the turbine in a pipe called a penstock. This penstock is built at an angle that allows the water to travel downward with force.

A dam ensures that the water falls a good distance in order to build up force. A lot of water above it will help to push it down. The more force behind the water, the faster it will turn the turbine and generator to generate electricity.

You probably noticed that the water in your set-up didn't push out with much force from the top hole, and that the bottom hole had the greatest force. Dams are built to use this to their advantage, but they're also built to make sure the water level is maintained whenever possible to maximize the force of the water.

UNIT 04 | USING ENERGY

IMAGINE HOW MUCH ENERGY YOU USE EVERY DAY. You wake up to an alarm powered by electricity, you charge your phone, you take a shower with hot water that is heated by electricity or natural gas, you eat breakfast, and you take a bus to school. These are only a small part of your day's energy use. The average citizen in North America uses about as much energy as is stored in 6 to 8 gallons (22 to 30 liters) of gasoline each day!

There are many ways we can use energy. A large percentage of the energy we use goes into transportation—transporting us in our personal or public vehicles, and transporting our goods from production facilities to points of sale. Another big chunk of the energy we use goes toward generating electricity to power our cell phones, computers, televisions, refrigerators, lights, and much more. The rest of our energy goes into keeping us comfortable in our homes and producing heat to make more goods. The labs in this unit will demonstrate the ways in which we consume or use energy each day, and how we're able to take energy sources like wind, petroleum, and biomass and turn them into energy to fuel our days and nights.

Light it up with a closed circuit in Lab 29!

LAB 26

PRETZEL POWER

TIME:
30 minutes

PERSON POWER:
All Hands on Deck! This activity is much more fun with a few friends, and they may come in handy for round two!

We use a good amount of energy each day, just to get from point A to point B. Most of our vehicles run on petroleum products, like gasoline and diesel fuel. Some of our vehicles are more efficient than others and allow us to go further on less fuel. The number of miles we can travel per gallon of gas (MPG) is a common description used to tell how efficient a vehicle may be. In this lab, you'll be able to get good idea of how to compare a vehicle's MPG rating as you try and get "around town" on a few gallons of gasoline!

Fig. 4: Have all the participants meet at home base with their cards and pretzels.

Fig 1: Place ten pretzels in a sandwich bag.

Fig. 2: Tape the home sign at your base.

MATERIALS

→ **pretzels**
→ **resealable plastic sandwich bag**
→ **construction paper**
→ **marker**
→ **tape**
→ **3" x 5" (7.6 x 12.7 cm) index cards**
→ **Internet access**

1. Place ten pretzels in a sandwich bag. Prepare one bag for each person who is participating (fig. 1).

2. Make three signs on construction paper: one labeled "Home," one labeled "Downtown," and one labeled "Across Town."

3. Select a large, open area. Tape the Home sign at a location that you will designate as your home base or starting point (fig. 2). Walk 50 steps (heel to toe) from home base, and tape the Downtown sign up so all crew members can see it. Walk another 50 steps (heel to toe) and tape the Across Town sign up for all to see. The Across Town sign should be about 100 steps away from Home. Don't tell anyone how far away is the signs are from each other!

4. Give each person an index card. Have them visit www.fueleconomy.gov and look up *any* car they might like to drive. Each person should record the car's name, model year, miles per gallon, type of fuel required, and number of passengers it can hold (fig. 3). If you pick a Flex Fuel Vehicle (FFV), select only one fuel you will use—gasoline or E85—and record the mileage.

ENERGY EXPLAINED

Vehicles do different amounts of work depending on what they're hauling and how they're constructed. The amount of work they must do is related to how much energy they'll use—or how much fuel they may burn. Lately, cars and trucks have been improving a lot in efficiency, meaning they travel more miles on one gallon of fuel. Trucks and sport utility vehicles (SUVs) use more fuel because they are often larger and made of durable parts to haul extra weight.

Sedans and compact cars often use less fuel because they are smaller and lighter. Sports cars and luxury cars may be made of lighter or higher-tech materials, but their engines are often high performance. This means they're meant to go very fast, use lots of power, and run with lots of accessories, all of which mean using more fuel more quickly. The kind of vehicle you purchase might require balancing looks, cost, function, and MPG rating. If you do a lot of traveling, you'll spend more to run a car that gets poor mileage.

If anyone selected a hybrid or battery-electric vehicle, they may have seen the notation MPGe. Since these cars do not run on traditional fuels, their mileage is reported as an equivalent. These cars typically have a very high MPG rating. But, battery-electric vehicles have one catch—their batteries must be recharged every so many miles. When purchasing these cars, it is important to pay attention to the range of the battery.

Fig. 3: Give each person an index card to write down his or her selected car's name, year, miles per gallon, type of fuel, and number of passengers.

5. Have all the participants join you at home base with their cards and their bags of pretzels (fig. 4). Make sure everyone waits to start snacking! Everyone will get a chance to eat the pretzels!

6. Each person will try to go from Home to Downtown and back using the car they have selected and only 5 gallons of fuel. Each pretzel in the bag represents one gallon of fuel, and each step they take, (heel to toe), will equal one mile traveled. Each person should eat one pretzel and take the appropriate number of steps (heel to toe) as listed on his or her car's MPG rating before eating the next pretzel. Aim to get from home to downtown and back on 5 gallons of fuel. *Example: If your car has an MPG rating of 15 miles per gallon, eat a pretzel and take fifteen steps.* Do you have any fuel remaining? Save it for future trips!

Fig. 5: After everyone has eaten five pretzels, look around. Were there any cars that didn't make it?

7. After everyone has eaten five pretzels (used five gallons), take a look around. Were there any cars that didn't make it (fig. 5)? Are there similarities between cars that made it and cars that didn't? Were there any cars that didn't even use five pretzels?

8. Have everyone start from Home again. This time, you want to make it from Home to Across Town and back Home again. Can you do it with the pretzels left in your bag? For those who know they won't make it, can you carpool? Join a group to share pretzels, but be careful—pick a car for all to ride in, but make sure you have no more than the maximum number of passengers. You wouldn't want to get a ticket!

LAB 27

ELECTROMAGWHAT?

TIME:
30 minutes

PERSON POWER:
No Sweat!

SAFETY IS KEY:
The battery set-up can get hot! Use caution, and if the wire or battery begins to feel hot, detach the wire from the battery and allow both to cool before continuing with the lab. Be sure to disconnect the wire from the battery when you're finished! If the ends of the wire are not exposed, have an adult use wire strippers to strip the ends about ½" to 1" (1.2 to 2.5 cm).

Fig. 5: Place the nail above the paper clips and lift.

Would you be lost without electricity? Possibly. Try and think of all the things you can do because you have the ability to flip a switch or plug in a device. Electricity wouldn't be possible without a few items—magnets, metals, and motion. In fact, electricity and magnetism are intricately related. In this lab, you'll experiment with electricity and magnets to see how they are related and allow us to do cool things!

MATERIALS

→ 3' (91 cm) piece of insulated copper wire (22 gauge), with ends exposed
→ compass
→ large steel nail
→ 9-volt battery
→ metal paper clips with no coating

1. Move the wire piece over the compass (fig. 1). Do you see the compass needle move?

2. Wrap the middle of the piece of wire around the large nail ten times so that it looks like a spring. Try to keep the coils from crossing or touching each other (fig. 2).

3. Attach the wire to the 9-volt battery terminals by wrapping each end around the metal contacts in a loop shape (fig. 3).

4. Move the compass near the wire-wrapped nail (fig. 4). Do you see the compass needle move? Which direction does it move? What have you done to the nail?

Fig. 1: Move the wire over the compass.

Fig. 2: Wrap the middle of the piece of wire around the nail ten times.

Fig. 3: Attach the wire to the 9-volt battery.

Fig. 4: Move the compass near the wire-wrapped nail.

5. Place a stack of paper clips on the table. Touch the end of the nail to the paper clips and lift. What do you see (fig. 5)?

6. Remove the ends of the wire from the battery.

7. Move the nail over the compass. Does the compass needle move now? Does it move in the same direction? Try again with only the coil of wire.

8. Place the nail above the paper clips and lift. Does the nail lift the paper clips now? Try it again with just the coil.

NOW TRY THIS!

Experiment with ways to lift more paper clips. What could you alter in your experiment to make a stronger electromagnet?

ENERGY EXPLAINED

Compasses are made with a magnetic needle. This needle is able to tell you which direction you're going because its magnetic field is responding to the magnetic field of the Earth. Magnetic fields are created by tiny spinning electrons!

Batteries create electricity when they are connected in a loop with a device and wires. Electrons flow out of the battery because chemicals react with the metals in the battery to make electricity. As this electricity flows through the wire, the electrons spin and form a magnetic field. This magnetic field in the wire causes the electrons in the nail to spin in the same way and become magnetized! This is why the nail wrapped with wire was able to pick up paper clips and move the compass.

The nail may have continued to pick up paper clips and move the needle after you unwrapped the wire because it was permanently magnetized! The coil may not work as effectively.

LAB 28

GENERATE THIS

TIME:
1 hour

PERSON POWER:
Grab a Crew Member!

SAFETY IS KEY:
Use caution when cutting cardboard and poking holes with nails. The model generates a small amount of voltage, but there is no shock risk.

Electricity and magnetism work together. With this relationship, we can use a very important device, called a generator. Let's build a generator and watch how magnets, motion, and metal wire can help generate electricity!

Fig. 9: Twist the wires and spin the nail.

Fig. 1: Make marks across the cardboard at the specified dimensions.

Fig. 2: Carefully score the cardboard on the lines between the numbered sections so they fold easily.

Fig. 3: Wrap the magnet wire clockwise around the box.

MATERIALS

→ 12" x 3" (30 cm x 8 cm) piece of cardboard
→ metric ruler
→ marker
→ sharp scissors
→ push pin
→ long nail
→ 2 ceramic bar magnets
→ 30-gauge magnet wire spool
→ sandpaper
→ LED single bulb
→ masking tape
→ glue or hot glue gun

1. Cut the piece of cardboard to the dimensions specified below. Use the ruler to measure and make marks across your piece of cardboard (fig. 1). Starting from the left edge, make a mark at 2⅛" (5.4 cm). Move over another 1¾" (4.4 cm) and make a mark. Move over another 2⅛" (5.4 cm) and make a mark. Move over another 1⅞" (4.7 cm) and make a mark. Move over another 2⅛" (5.4 cm) and make a mark. Make sure to mark the bottom edge of the cardboard, too, and draw lines from top to bottom to make rectangular sections.

Example:

← 5.4 cm →	← 4.4 cm →	← 5.4 cm →	← 4.7 cm →	← 5.4 cm →	
1	**2**	**3**	**4**	**5**	extra material
← 5.4 cm →	← 4.4 cm →	← 5.4 cm →	← 4.7 cm →	← 5.4 cm →	

2. Cut off the extra material but do not discard it. You'll need it later. Number the remaining sections 1 through 5.

3. In sections 2 and 4, make a mark ⅞" (2.2 cm) in from the left edge and 1⅝" (4 cm) up from the bottom. This is where the nail will be inserted. Insert the push pin into the markings, and then push the nail through to enlarge the holes. Make sure the holes are actually a bit larger than the nail so that the cardboard can spin freely around the nail.

Fig. 4: Tape the wires in place.

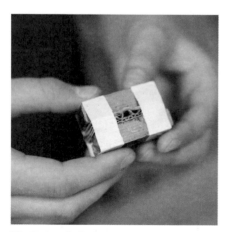

Fig. 5: Stack the magnets lengthwise.

4. Using the scissors and the ruler, carefully score the cardboard on the lines between the numbered sections so they fold easily (fig. 2). Be careful not to cut the whole way through the cardboard. Starting with section one, fold the sections into a box, with section 5 overlapping section 1. Hold a magnet inside the box. If it doesn't fit, make it a bit wider. Once it's wide enough, tape the box together.

5. Tear off six pieces of masking tape, each 2" to 3" (5 to 7.6 cm) long, and have them ready.

6. Leaving an 8" (20.3 cm) tail hanging off, begin to wrap the magnet wire clockwise around the box about 1" (2.5 cm) below the nail hole (fig. 3). Tape the first wrap in place. Wrap it 200 more times in this area below the hole. Make sure you do not

Fig. 6: Slide the nail into the spacer.

Fig. 7: Scrape the colored coating off the wire tails.

Fig. 8: Twist the wires around the bulb ends.

wrap so tightly that the box collapses, but make sure your wire wraps are close together. *Do not cut* the wire. Use a piece of tape to secure the 200 wraps in place below the hole.

7. String the wire above the hole (do not cut it). Tape it in place. Continue to wrap clockwise above the hole for an additional 200 wraps. Again, keep the wraps close together, but do not cover the holes. Tape these wraps in place, too (fig. 4).

8. Leave an 8" (20 cm) tail of wire attached to the last wrap above the hole. You should now have two tails, each hanging from one set of wraps—one above and one below the nail hole. Cut the wire.

9. Stack the two magnets together lengthwise so you know which ends attract (fig. 5). Place a ¾" (2 cm) piece of cardboard between the magnets to act as a spacer. Make sure the nail can slide into the corrugation between the two magnets. Tape the magnets together so they will stay put during spinning.

10. Holding the magnets in place inside the box, slide the nail through one side of the box, into the spacer between the magnets, and out the other side of the box (fig. 6). Spin the nail to make sure the magnets move freely.

11. Using sandpaper, scrape the colored coating off the wire tails, so no color remains (fig. 7). Twist the wires around the lightbulb ends (fig. 8). Spin the nail (fig. 9). Can you get your bulb to light? What happens when you spin it faster or slower?

ENERGY EXPLAINED

Metals contain an electric charge that doesn't stay put—it can move around. When a circle of metal wire gets near a magnetic field, the electric charge (or electrons) tries to move. As the magnets in your generator move around in a circle, the electric charges in the wires try to do the same thing. Moving electrons are electricity!

When the wires are connected to a device, like the bulb, in a closed loop, the electrons flow into the bulb to light it and back around again. If you stop the magnet motion, the electron motion stops in the wire, and the bulb goes out. This is a generator. Believe it or not, generators at electric power facilities work much the same way. Of course their generators are much larger, with larger coils of wire, and much bigger, stronger magnets. Once they get moving near each other, you've got electricity!

LAB 29

LIGHT IT UP!

TIME:
5–20 minutes

PERSON POWER:
No Sweat!

SAFETY IS KEY:
Be careful when you touch the foil to the battery. The foil may become hot.

We use energy to create electricity, which, in turn, powers many of the things we use every day. Most of our electricity is generated by one of two devices: a generator or a battery. Generators move magnets near coils of wire to get electrons flowing. Batteries use the chemical reaction of an acid with two different metals to make electrons move, like in the electromagnets activity.

Electricity travels in closed circuits. Electrons must have a complete path made of wires running from the generator or battery into devices and back to the generator or battery in order to have a continuous flow. If the circuit is open or broken, electricity cannot flow. When you flip a light switch, you are opening and closing the pathway for electricity to flow from power lines into your lightbulbs. But can we make a lightbulb light with a battery? What would the circuit look like?

Fig. 2: Make a closed circuit.

MATERIALS

→ aluminum foil
→ scissors
→ masking tape
→ D-cell battery
→ mini incandescent or LED flashlight bulb (0.5–3 volts/0.2 amps)

1. Cut a piece of aluminum foil into strips at least 4" (10 cm) long. The width of the strips can vary (fig. 1).

Fig. 1: Cut the foil into strips.

Fig. 3: Experiment with different widths of wire.

Fig. 4: Try to make a complete circuit.

QUICK TIP

Electricity needs to have a path into every device and back out to the battery in order to flow. In this lab, electricity travels through the strip, into the bulb, out of the bulb, and back to the battery.

2. Select one foil strip. Make a closed electrical circuit by taping one end of the strip to one end of the battery, and the other end of the strip to the opposite end of the battery (fig. 2). Feel the battery and the strip of foil at different spots. What do you notice?

3. Remove the tape and foil to disassemble the circuit.

4. Experiment with different widths and lengths of foil and pay attention to the similarities or differences you observe (fig. 3). Disassemble each piece after observation.

5. Using one foil strip of your choice, the battery, and the light-bulb, try to make a complete circuit so that the foil connects to both the battery and the bulb (fig. 4). You can do it! Check out the Quick Tip to get you started.

6. Try several different arrangements of the circuit, and alter the foil size and shape. Which configuration makes the bulb light the brightest?

ENERGY EXPLAINED

Electrons will flow only if a circuit is closed. You have probably experienced this before with batteries—if they are not properly inserted, electricity can't flow through and the device will not turn on. The same thing is true in your house if you trip a breaker or blow a fuse—these devices allow electricity to flow through. If too much electricity flows through, they might trip, causing the circuit to open. This is built in for safety purposes! With the lightbulb, you needed the foil to touch the battery at one spot. The electricity had to go through the foil and into the bulb *and* back out into the battery. If you don't allow the electrons to flow back out of the bulb and into the battery, your circuit is not closed and the bulb will not light!

LAB 30

CHIP COMBUSTION

TIME:
45 minutes

PERSON POWER:
Grab a Crew Member! For this activity, it's best that you have an adult crew member available.

MESS ALERT!
This lab is not messy, but since you will be burning food, it is best to conduct the activity in a well-ventilated area or outdoors.

SAFETY IS KEY:
You'll need an adult to supervise this lab. You will be puncturing an aluminum can and using fire. Use goggles, an oven mitt to handle the cans, and be very careful.

Living things need energy. We use a lot of energy to move and grow each day. Even if we don't grow bigger each day, we still grow new cells! Living things need chemical energy to make this happen. Our chemical energy comes from the food we eat. Much of this food got its energy from the sun. We have to release this chemical energy in some way in order to make use of it, so our bodies digest it to break it down and we burn calories. Let's burn some food and see what happens!

Fig. 8: Allow the food to burn completely.

Fig. 1: Carefully make four holes in the sides of the drink can.

Fig. 2: Slide a skewer into one hole and out the hole across from it.

Fig. 3: Insert the thermometer in the can and take a reading.

MATERIALS

→ can opener
→ empty, clean aluminum drink can
→ empty, clean metal coffee can
→ sharp scissors and/or screwdriver
→ 2 metal skewers
→ water
→ glass thermometer or candy thermometer (a digital thermometer will not work)
→ metal paper clip
→ cork
→ potato chip, cheese curl, or similar snack food
→ long-handled lighter

1. Using the can opener, make sure the larger can is completely open at the top and the bottom.

2. Using the scissors and/or the screwdriver, *carefully* make four holes in the sides of the aluminum drink can, ½" (1.3 cm) from the top edge (fig. 1). The holes should be evenly spaced and directly across from one another.

ENERGY EXPLAINED

Food provides us with energy in the form of calories. Those calories come from the simple sugars, muscles, fat, and other nutrients inside the food we eat. All of those nutrients came originally from the sun during the process of photosynthesis, and in order for us to use them as energy, our body must break them down. When we're doing this, we're burning calories!

In this activity, you burned food to see how it can provide energy. As the food burned, its chemical energy turned into thermal energy and caused the temperature of the water to rise. In our bodies, energy transformations occur like this constantly—turning the chemical energy in our foods into thermal energy, motion energy, and even sound energy! Some foods have more energy in them based on how big they are or the types of nutrients in them. You built a calorimeter apparatus—a device used by nutritionists to determine how much energy is in a food item. Calorimeters measure the energy inside based on the amount of temperature change. This is how calorie content is calculated!

Fig. 4: Open a paper clip and insert the straight end into the piece of cork.

Fig. 5: Balance or spear the food onto the end of the paper clip.

3. Slide one metal skewer into one hole and out of the hole across from it. Slide the other skewer through the other hole and out the opposite side (fig. 2). The skewers should cross each other in the middle.

4. Place the larger can on a flat surface. Place the smaller can inside, making sure the skewers rest on the top edges of the larger can and that there is space between the bottom of the aluminum can and the flat surface to place the cork.

5. Pour ½ cup (118 ml) of water into the aluminum can through the hole in the top. Insert the thermometer in the can and take a temperature reading (fig. 3).

Fig. 6: Ask a partner to hold the drink can while you light the food.

Fig. 7: Place the smaller can down into the large can.

6. Make sure your cork will fit under the cans in your set-up. Cut the cork down if needed or lay it on its side. Partially open a paper clip and insert the straight end into the piece of cork (fig. 4). Leave a flat surface at the opposite end of the paper clip. This end of the paper clip will act as a stand on which to place the food you will burn.

7. Remove the small can from the larger can and keep it close by. Place the cork in the center of the larger can and rest or balance one snack item on the paper clip on top of it. Unfold or adjust the clip to help keep the food from moving. Spear the food, if you must (fig. 5)!

8. Ask a partner to hold the aluminum drink can nearby as you light the food on fire (fig. 6). As soon as you light the food, place the smaller can down into the large can, so it is resting as it did before, but just above the burning food (fig. 7). Allow the food to burn completely, and then stir the water and examine how the temperature of the water changed (fig. 8). Why did it change? Would a different piece of food produce different results?

NOW TRY THIS!

Figure out how many calories were in your food! A simple equation for calories = volume of water (in ml) x temperature change (in degrees C). You started with 118 ml of water. Multiply by the temperature change, and that should roughly equal the number of calories in the item burned!

Try comparing it to the nutrition labels and try it with different foods.

UNIT 05
SAVING ENERGY: CONSERVE AND PRESERVE

USING ENERGY TO POWER OUR LIVES means we rely on many energy sources to get us through the day. We make choices about how we use energy without thinking much about it. We choose to keep our laptops on and plugged in when they're not in use, but we might choose to make sure we turn the lights off when we leave a room. Instead of walking, we might drive a short distance to buy a few things, but then we decide to carpool to our soccer game. These choices factor into the total amount of energy we use and have economic and environmental impacts.

When we play a video game, we pay for the electricity that powers our game console. Most of the electricity in North America is generated from nonrenewable energy sources, many of which must be burned to generate steam. This process can release emissions that have environmental impacts.

There are many things we can do to use less energy and to use it more wisely. These actions are called energy conservation and energy efficiency. Energy conservation is an action, behavior, or decision that results in using less energy. Examples of energy conservation include turning the lights off when you leave the room, using public transportation rather than a personal vehicle, and recycling or reusing products. Energy efficiency is the use of a technology or device that helps us to do the same work with less energy. Examples of energy efficiency include replacing old lightbulbs with newer, more efficient bulbs, or buying a more fuel-efficient car with a higher miles-per-gallon (MPG) rating. Energy conservation is easy to practice without much extra cost. Energy-efficient technologies can be flashy and high tech, and they can sometimes be expensive.

You can't really have efficiency without conservation; they must work together. If you have a fancy hybrid car, but don't know how to use the energy-saving features, then the car isn't going to make much of a difference. By thinking about our energy use, measuring and observing our actions, and changing our behaviors, we can make noticeable changes in our personal energy expenses and also preserve our environment. The labs in this unit will give you an opportunity to observe and measure ways that you use energy in your home and day-to-day activities, as well as to identify ways to reduce energy consumption and care for the environment.

What happens when there's too much carbon dioxide? Find out in Lab 39.

INSULATORS TO THE RESCUE!

TIME:
30 minutes

PERSON POWER:
No Sweat!

SAFETY IS KEY:
You will need hot water for this activity. The water does not need to be boiling, just hot. Be careful when heating and transferring water to the cans. Ask an adult for help if needed.

Keeping our homes at a comfortable temperature is usually the highest household energy expense. This lab will explore how insulation can help hold temperature in your home.

⎘ MATERIALS

→ 5 empty, clean aluminum cans
→ bubble wrap
→ cotton batting
→ polyester batting
→ foam craft sheet
→ masking tape
→ rubber bands
→ hot water
→ saucepan or teapot
→ measuring cup
→ 5 cotton balls
→ digital kitchen thermometer (one is good, but five are better!)
→ timer
→ notebook and pencil

Fig. 3: Record the starting temperature of each can.

1. Select four of the cans. Wrap one with bubble wrap, one with cotton batting, one with polyester batting, and one with craft foam. Secure the insulation on each with tape and rubber bands (fig. 1). Leave the fifth can unwrapped as your experimental control.

2. Use a measuring cup to fill all five cans with hot water through their top openings (fig. 2). Quickly wedge a cotton ball into each opening to keep air from leaking out.

3. Use the thermometer(s) to take a temperature reading of the water in each can, and then quickly replace the cotton ball. Record the starting temperature of each can (fig. 3). Which one do you think will stay hottest the longest?

Fig. 1: Wrap the cans to insulate them.

Fig. 2: Use a measuring cup to fill all five cans.

Fig. 4: Record the temperature of the water every two minutes.

4. Set the timer for two minutes. Record the temperature of the water in each can every two minutes for twenty minutes (fig. 4). Which can keeps its temperature the longest? Which is the best insulator and which is the worst? Ask an adult if your home uses insulation and find out where it is.

5. During the two-minute waits between each reading, you can take the temperature of your home in each room. Doesn't this require a different type of thermometer? Will it give you an accurate reading in two minutes? Are there some rooms that are warmer or cooler than others? What are some reasons for temperature changes between rooms?

Thermostat Tug of War

Residents in a house often disagree on what is a comfortable temperature. Why not let your bills decide the winner! Did you know that adjusting or programming your thermostat is an easy way to save a little money each month? When you're not at home during the day, set the temperature lower (in colder weather) or higher (in warmer weather) so your system doesn't have to work as hard. You can adjust your thermostat back to a comfortable temperature when you return home, or program it so that it's working upon your arrival. Even an adjustment of 2 to 3 degrees each day can make a difference of 10 percent on your energy bill!

ENERGY EXPLAINED

Insulation helps us keep our homes at a comfortable temperature by resisting thermal energy flow through conduction and convection. Air always flows from areas of high temperature to low temperature. So, in the winter, warm air wants to flow toward the cold air until there is no difference in temperature. It can flow through walls, windows, doors, and even through the roof. This accounts for different temperatures in different rooms of your house. Your heater must compensate for all the warm air lost. Insulation helps to wrap your home in a blanket to keep warm and cold air where you want them!

Insulation also works the same way in warm climates—sealing in the cool air and keeping the hot air outside! Different materials have different insulating capacities, just as you witnessed in this lab.

DRAFT DETECTIVE

Fig. 4: Play detective in your home with your streamer.

The air in your home naturally tries to leak out, and fresh air tries to come back in. This can be a problem when we pay to heat or cool the air in our homes to keep us comfy. How does the air get in and out? In this lab, you will explore the places where air might leak with a fun, easy-to-assemble tool! Put on your Sherlock Holmes hat and get ready for detective work!

1. Cut a strip of paper about 2" (5 cm) wide and 3" to 4" (7.5 to 10 cm) long (fig. 1).

2. Tape one end of the paper to the end of the pencil, like a streamer with a handle (fig. 2).

3. Start by holding the taped portion of your streamer in front of a fan to watch its movement (fig. 3). If you don't have a fan handy, blow on it with different amounts of air pressure to make sure it moves and that you can see differences in movement.

4. Travel around your home with your streamer and play detective (fig. 4). Hold the streamer up to window seams (bottom, top, and sides), door seams (bottom, top, and sides), and electrical outlet covers (fig. 5). Did you find any locations where you can feel air flowing or see air moving the streamer?

TIME:
15–20 minutes

PERSON POWER:
No Sweat!

✎ MATERIALS

→ **crepe paper or toilet paper**
→ **scissors**
→ **ruler**
→ **pencil, wood dowel, or screwdriver**
→ **tape**
→ **electric fan**

Fig. 1: Cut a piece of paper 3" to 4" (7.6 to 10 cm) long.

Fig. 2: Tape one end of the paper to the pencil.

Fig. 3: Hold the streamer in front of a fan.

Fig. 5: Hold the streamer up to window and door seams.

COOL CAREER—CERTIFIED ENERGY MANAGER (CEM) OR BUILDING ANALYST (BA)

CEMs and BAs are energy detectives for homes or businesses. They help customers by traveling around, under, above, and into homes to figure out where energy might be wasted. They are specially trained to look for how heat, air, and moisture move through a home and how electrical devices consume energy. CEMs and BAs look for clues by comparing utility bills, inspecting the home with special tools, and taking measurements. They are often able to help a home or business owner save money without spending much money at all!

ENERGY EXPLAINED

Even if your home is insulated, air can still leak out and sneak in. Some spots that can't be covered by insulation are natural sites for air leaks. Electrical outlets and light-switch covers are common locations of small drafts. This is usually because those areas have gaps in insulation to allow for the electrical components behind them. The same thing occurs where lighting fixtures are installed into ceilings and walls! Doors and windows may not seal tightly in their frames because of the way they were installed, or because the house has settled over time. You may have noticed leaks in these areas, too.

What can be done about these air leaks? New windows and doors aren't always in the budget, but a quick fix could be to use caulking or foam strips with a sticky backing (weather stripping) in the areas where leaks occur. Easy-to-install foam gaskets can also be put in place around doors and behind light switch and outlet covers!

LAB 33

LIGHTEN UP!

TIME:
30 minutes to an hour

PERSON POWER:
No Sweat! or Grab a Crew Member!

SAFETY IS KEY:
Have an adult present if changing or removing bulbs from their fixtures. Be extra careful because bulbs may be hot. Also, bulbs are made of glass, which can be dangerous if broken. CFL bulbs contain mercury, which can be harmful to the skin and lungs if the bulb is broken.

Fig. 1: Go on a lightbulb scavenger hunt in your home.

In your home, up to 15 percent of the electricity you use goes to your lightbulbs. Lightbulbs are small, but very important, tools to make your day (and night) productive! There are many different lightbulbs available to use in the home. How are they similar and how are they different? Are some bulbs better energy savers than others? This activity will focus on four basic types of bulbs: incandescent, halogen incandescent, compact fluorescent (CFL), and light emitting diode (LED).

	INCANDESCENT BULB	HALOGEN	COMPACT FLUORESCENT (CFL)	LIGHT EMITTING DIODE (LED)
Brightness →	850 lumens	850 lumens	850 lumens	850 lumens
Life of Bulb →	1,000 hours	3,000 hours	10,000 hours	25,000 hours
Energy Use →	60 watts = 0.06 KW	43 watts = 0.043 KW	13 watts = 0.013 KW	12 watts = 0.012 KW
Price per Bulb →	$0.50	$3.00	$3.00	$8.00

All bulbs provide about 850 lumens of light.

	COST OF BULB	INCANDESCENT BULB	HALOGEN	COMPACT FLUORESCENT (CFL)	LIGHT EMITTING DIODE (LED)
	Life of Bulb (how long it will light)	1,000 hours	3,000 hours	10,000 hours	25,000 hours
	Number of Bulbs to Get 25,000 Hours				
x	Price per Bulb	$0.50	$3.00	$3.00	$8.00
=	Cost of Bulbs for 25,000 Hours of Light				
	COST OF ELECTRICITY	Incandescent Bulb	Halogen	Compact Fluorescent (CFL)	Light Emitting Diode (LED)
	Total Hours	25,000 hours	25,000 hours	25,000 hours	25,000 hours
x	Wattage	60 watts = 0.06 KW	43 watts = 0.043 KW	13 watts = 0.013 KW	12 watts = 0.012 KW
=	Total kWh Consumption				
x	Price of Electricity per kWh	$0.10	$0.10	$0.10	$0.10
=	Cost of Electricity				
	LIFE CYCLE COST	Incandescent Bulb	Halogen	Compact Fluorescent (CFL)	Light Emitting Diode (LED)
	Cost of Bulbs				
=	Cost of Electricity				
=	Life Cycle Cost				

MATERIALS

→ lightbulbs and lamps
→ thermometers
→ calculator

1. Go on a scavenger hunt in your home and around the outside of your home (fig. 1). Take count all the lightbulbs you see.

2. Using the pictures, and the help of an adult, look at the bulbs closely to classify each as incandescent, halogen, CFL, or LED (fig. 2). Which type of bulbs do you use most? Is there a reason some bulbs are used in certain spaces?

Fig. 2: Classify all the bulbs that you find.

Fig. 3: Hold a thermometer a few centimeters (1 inch) away from each lit bulb.

3. Turn on each bulb that you find. Hold or place a thermometer a few centimeters away from it (fig. 3). Does the temperature change for each? Is there a difference in temperature for each type of bulb? Don't forget to turn off each bulb again!

4. Why do people suggest we switch our light bulbs to be more efficient? Try a comparison activity! One LED bulb can last up to 25,000 hours. The cost to buy the bulb is around $8.00, but we must also pay for the electricity to power the bulb for 25,000 hours. The price of the electricity plus the original price of the bulb is called the life-cycle cost. Complete the calculations in the table on page 109 to find out the life-cycle cost for each type of bulb. Which is the better buy overall? What happens if the cost of a CFL or LED goes up by $5? What happens if these bulbs become cheaper?

5. How much could you save by switching all the bulbs in one room of your home? Your entire home?

Conductors, insulators, and semiconductors

CONDUCTORS, INSULATORS, AND SEMICONDUCTORS...OH MY!

Conductors are materials that allow electricity and thermal energy to move through them. Many metals are good conductors. If they touch something hot, they too become hot.

Insulators are materials that stop the flow of electricity or thermal energy. Rubber is used for the handles of cooking utensils and as the coating for wires because it is a good insulator and doesn't get hot.

Semiconductors are materials that aren't really good conductors and aren't really good insulators, either. But semiconductors are useful because they allow us to direct how electricity moves through the circuit. Semiconductors can make a circuit smaller and more efficient than if a conductor was used. Silicon is an example of a common semiconductor material found in many electronic devices and even LED bulbs.

ENERGY EXPLAINED

Incandescent bulbs create light by sending electricity into the bulb and through a filament. This filament becomes very hot and glows as electricity flows back out the other side. The glowing filament can light up a whole room, but it also can become very hot. Almost all incandescent bulbs have been phased out by the government, but they can still be found in homes and businesses.

Halogen bulbs work the same way as incandescent bulbs. The filament in a halogen bulb is enclosed in a capsule of halogen gas. This gas extends the life of the filament and allows the filament to get hotter without the bulb releasing as much thermal energy (heat). These are often called energy-saving incandescent bulbs and look very much like a traditional incandescent bulb.

CFLs provide the same amount of light as incandescent bulbs, but they produce far less thermal energy (heat) and use much less electricity. CFLs work by sending electric current into the bulb. The bulb is filled with gases and a small amount of mercury. The walls of the bulb are coated with phosphor. The mercury conducts electricity and emits UV radiation, which fluoresces (glows) when it hits the phosphor-coated walls of the bulb.

LEDs provide similar light, but they use even less electricity than CFLs. LEDs allow light to be produced because they are made of special materials called semiconductors. LEDs have been around for many years in exit signs and on remote controls, but they can now be placed in everything from the lights in your home to the giant screen at a stadium.

SOLAR WATER HEATER

Fig. 2: Record the temperature of the water in both cans.

TIME:
30 minutes

PERSON POWER:
No Sweat!

📎 MATERIALS

→ 2 empty soup cans
→ black paint
→ paintbrush
→ water (room temperature)
→ measuring cup
→ 2 digital thermometers
→ notebook and pencil
→ plastic wrap
→ rubber bands
→ timer

Another big expense for homes and businesses is heating water. Every family has that *one* person who takes long, hot showers! Using less hot water is easy to do, but, if you want to go high efficiency, a solar water heater is a great fix. In this lab, you will explore how a solar water heater can help heat water in a home. Get ready to take in some vitamin D while you wait—you'll need a sunny day for this lab!

1. Remove the labels from the soup cans. Paint one of the cans black and allow it to dry. Leave the other can shiny.

2. Fill both cans with ⅔ cup (158 ml) of water so they are halfway full. Make sure you have the same amount of water in each (fig. 1).

3. Take the temperature of the water in both cans and record it (fig. 2).

4. Cover both cans with plastic wrap and secure it with a rubber band (fig. 3).

5. Take the cans outside and place them in direct sunlight. Record the temperature again every minute for fifteen minutes (fig. 4). Poke the digital thermometer through the plastic wrap and into the water. Record the temperatures. Which can shows the greatest temperature increase?

Fig. 1: Fill both cans with water; make sure you have the same amount in each.

Fig. 3: Cover both cans with plastic wrap.

Fig. 4: Take the temperature of the water every 15 minutes.

ENERGY EXPLAINED

Radiant energy (sunlight) can heat things. Anything that uses solar energy to trap thermal energy is called a solar collector. Your car on a sunny day, a solar cooker, and a greenhouse are great examples of solar collectors.

Solar water heaters include a solar collector. In this lab, you made two solar collectors—one shiny and one black. You should have seen the temperature in both containers increase when placed in the sunlight. But the black can would show the greatest increase because dark surfaces absorb more radiant energy from the sun.

Solar water heaters are often mounted on a roof, where solar energy exposure is ample. Some portion of the solar water heater is usually black to allow the water to be warmed by the radiant energy absorbed. Modern solar water heaters incorporate a small tank and a series of tubes that allow water to travel through. The tubes themselves are dark in color or are mounted on a black collection surface with reflectors on the side.

Was your water hot enough to shower in? Probably not after fifteen minutes. So how does this save you energy? Water coming into your home from underground water lines is cooler than you'd like for a shower. By piping this water into a solar collector, the water is heated using the sun's energy. If the water still needs to be hotter, a back-up water heater will heat it further, but it will use only a little energy since the water has already been warmed by the sun! Many homes with solar water heaters also have a regular water heater that allows them to store hot water from the solar collector and create hot water when it's not sunny. However, these homes often need a much smaller water heater than homes that do not have solar water heating.

LAB 35

WATTS IT ALL ABOUT?

TIME:
30 minutes
(or as long as you'd like)

PERSON POWER:
Grab a Crew Member!
Math is more fun with
a friend, plus it's helpful
to have a second set
of eyes when moving
devices and looking
for information. Make
sure you ask permission
before unplugging and
moving any devices
someone might be using!

SAFETY IS KEY:
When unplugging
devices, always pull on
the plug itself. Never
unplug a device by
grabbing and pulling
the cord.

Electronics can use a *load* of energy. In fact, "load" is often the term used to describe any pluggable electronic device. Can you count the number of items plugged in at your home right now? It would likely be pretty difficult, since so many of our appliances, machines, and personal devices are pluggables. We use energy from these devices in units called watts. We can figure out how much each item costs us to use by doing some detective work and math. Break out your calculator: this lab will allow you to calculate just how much energy each item in your home uses and how much it costs you each year!

Fig. 1: Find the nameplates on five devices in your home.

📎 MATERIALS

→ **pluggable appliances and devices (easy-to-move items are good choices)**
→ **camera or camera phone**
→ **electricity bill (optional)**
→ **notebook and pencil**
→ **calculator**

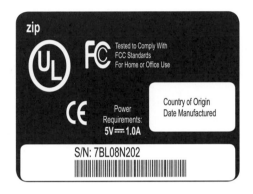

PART I

1. Every machine that runs on electricity in your home has a nameplate on it that includes information about amps (A), volts (V), and sometimes watts (W). Nameplates are often stickers or stamps on the surface that look like the picture shown above. Often these can be found on the bottom or backs of devices, but sometimes you have to look closely. Find the nameplates on five devices in your home (fig. 1). Use caution and unplug devices, if needed. Easy options include: television, game console, laptop and/or laptop charger, hair dryer, toaster, vacuum cleaner, and alarm clock.

2. Take a picture of each device's nameplate and any information printed on the device related to its amps, volts, or watts (fig. 2). Sometimes, devices like vacuum cleaners and hair dryers tell you their wattage or amperage in big bold letters because it's important to the device's function.

3. Make a chart like the one on page 116. Record any information you see on each nameplate. For most items, you will see current and voltage, and maybe watts.

ENERGY EXPLAINED

Are you shocked? Shocked is probably not a good word choice when you're talking about electricity! But it can be interesting and eye opening to figure out the dollars and cents we need to operate our favorite devices. Using some devices may cost only a few dollars a year. It gets interesting, however, when you add up *all* the devices in your home. A single television may not cost much per year, but many people have several televisions. Adding all these devices together can account for a lot, especially when we consider that larger appliances use more energy and might be used all the time! The average family home uses about 900 kWh a month!

NOTE: A nameplate lists maximum ratings. Not all devices use the maximum at all times; many have cycles and processes that use small amounts of energy some of the time and larger amounts at other times. Special devices called Kill-A-Watt® meters can help determine exactly how much a device is using at any time.

Machine or appliance	Current (A)	Voltage (V)	Wattage (W)	Kilowatts (kW)	Hours Used per Day	Hours Used per Year	Cost per kWh	Total Cost

PART 2

1. To determine the cost to use each device, we need to figure out how many watts are used. If watts are not listed on the nameplate, you can calculate them by multiplying the current (amps) times the voltage. Record the wattage in the correct column.

2. We use many watts of electricity each month. Because of this, we are not billed for our energy use in watts. WATT? We're billed in a larger unit—kilowatt-hours. We can figure out our kilowatt hours too! First we have to turn watts into kilowatts. 1 kilowatt is equal to 1000 watts, so we must divide the wattage by 1000. Record this number in the kilowatts column.

3. To figure out how often we use a particular device, we might need to do some thinking or interviewing. Consider how many hours per day the device is plugged in, turned on, and in use. Ask a family member if you're unsure. Enter this number in the correct column.

4. Some items, like televisions or laptops, may be used on a daily basis. If an item gets used each day, multiply the hours per day by the number of days in a year (365) to find out the number of hours per year. If an appliance or device is used only a few times a year, multiply by the number of days it is actually used. Ask the family member who uses it for an estimate. Enter these figures in the correct column.

5. We are billed for our electrical use in kilowatt-hours (kWh). The average price throughout much of North America is 12 cents per kilowatt-hour, but the amount may be more or less where you live. Check your family's electricity bill to find your kWh cost. If you don't have a bill on hand, enter $0.12 in the cost column for the national average.

6. Now we must calculate the total cost (fig. 3). Since we are billed in kilowatt-hours, multiply the kilowatts column by the hours-per-year column times the cost-per-kWh column. This number will be the total cost for each device per year!

Fig. 2: Take a picture of each device's nameplate.

NOW TRY THiS!

Check out your home's electric meter at the beginning of the day. Go back and check it at the end of the day. How many kilowatt-hours were used? Make a list of all the items that were turned on in your house today that contribute to this consumption. Could you turn some things off and make the list smaller?

Fig. 3: Calculate the total cost.

LAB 36

FRIDGE FUN

Fig. 1: Place the thermometer in the glass on a shelf in the refrigerator.

TIME:
15 minutes, plus 5 minutes the next day

PERSON POWER:
No Sweat!

MATERIALS

→ **2 alcohol thermometers**
→ **water**
→ **drinking glass**
→ **dollar bill**

Is your refrigerator running? Well, you'd better go catch it! That joke is so old, but one thing is true: refrigerators are always running. In fact, the refrigerator typically consumes the most energy of all appliances in a home, because it's running all day, every day, keeping our food chilled and safe for eating. This lab will allow you to explore your refrigerator to make sure it is operating efficiently and not wasting energy.

TEST 1

1. Many refrigerators do not have actual thermostats; they have dials with settings that correspond to a temperature. Take note of the setting in your refrigerator.

2. Fill a drinking glass with warm water. Place the thermometer in the glass and position it on the shelf in the center of your refrigerator. Record the starting temperature (fig. 1).

3. Allow the thermometer to remain in place for twenty-four hours, and record the temperature again.

4. Now take note of the setting for your freezer. Place the second thermometer between two frozen food packages in the freezer (fig. 2). Allow it to remain for twenty-four hours before checking the temperature.

Fig. 2: Place the second thermometer between frozen foods in the freezer.

Fig. 3: Place a dollar bill half in the refrigerator and half out.

Fig. 4: Grasp the end of the dollar bill and pull it.

5. The recommended temperature for a refrigerator is 35°F to 38°F (1.6°C to 3.3°C). What is the temperature of the water in your refrigerator? How much did the water cool? The recommended setting for a freezer is 0°F (−17.7°C) Should you adjust your settings up or down? Try adjusting the settings by one notch each and repeat the tests. Setting the dial at too cold a temperature means you're wasting energy and money. Not setting the temperature cold enough, however, could mean your food is unsafe.

TEST 2

1. Refrigerators seal shut when we close them, thanks to the rubber gaskets around the door. Place a dollar bill half inside the refrigerator and half outside. Close the door (fig. 3).

2. Try to remove the dollar bill by grasping the end and gently pulling it (fig. 4). Avoid fast or abrupt jerking, as it could tear. Did the bill move? Is it easy or difficult to make it move? How do you think this helps or hurts your refrigerator?

NOW TRY THIS!

There's a common debate about refrigerators—to fill or not to fill? Well, that can depend on the fridge, how it cycles its refrigerant, and the number of times you open the door. Repeat test 1 when the refrigerator is full, and repeat it again when it is somewhat empty. Which works better to keep your water glass cold?

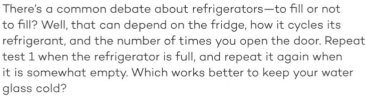

ENERGY EXPLAINED

Refrigerators cool our food and keep it cold by removing moisture and warm air from inside the fridge and sending it outside. Thermal energy always flows from high temperature to low temperature, so a refrigerator has to use a refrigerant to help it do its work. Since heat flows back into the cooled space, a refrigerator must keep running to pump that warmer air out.

Your refrigerator has seals, or gaskets, that help stop air leaks. Over time, these gaskets can wear out. Your dollar bill should not slide out easily. If it did, that means that warm air can enter easily. Replacing the gaskets is a cost-effective way to enhance your refrigerator's performance, but, so is minimizing the number of times you open the doors! The more and longer the door is open, the harder a refrigerator must work to keep food cool!

LAB 37

MONITOR A MONTH... (OR A WEEK)

TIME:
15 to 20 minutes each day for 1 week to 1 month

PERSON POWER:
No Sweat! But, it's definitely more interesting to work as a family, so if possible, Grab a Crew Member, or four, from your family!

Have you ever observed adults on a diet? They often record or write down *everything* they eat. It might seem annoying, but it helps them to understand easily where they could cut out something unnecessary or budget for times they might have to splurge. Well, when conserving energy and employing energy-efficient technologies to save energy, it's almost as if we're going on an energy diet! This long-term lab aims to allow you and your family to observe how you use energy. Will you be able to identify a few places where you can cut the fat?

 MATERIALS

→ notebook and pencil
→ thermometer
→ camera or camera phone
→ spreadsheet software (optional)

Fig. 1: Find your home's electrical meter and record the starting reading.

1. Decide as a group how many days of energy behaviors you will monitor. Pick a start day and time, as well as an end day and time.

2. Find your home's electric meter and record the starting reading (fig. 1). (If your meter is not digital, round the number down if the arrow is between two numbers). If your home uses natural gas, too, you may also wish to record the gas meter reading for this. Ask an adult for help with finding and reading the gas meter.

MONITORING SURVEY

A. Did we run the dishwasher? _____

     How many times? _____

     Was it completely full each time? _____

     What setting was used for each? _____

B. How many loads of laundry were done?

     What temperature was used for washing in each load? _____

     What temperature was used for rinsing in each load? _____

C. How many baths were taken? _____

D. How many showers were taken? _____

     How long (on average) was each shower? _____

E. Are we heating or cooling the house in this season? _____

     What temperature was the thermostat set to during the day? _____

     What temperature was the thermostat set to during the night? _____

     Were any windows open while the system was in use? _____

     What was the outdoor temperature (high) during the day? _____

     What was the outdoor temperature (low) at night? _____

     What was the weather like? _____

     Did we use fans or open windows today instead of heating or cooling? _____

     Did we open the blinds or close them during the day? _____

F. How many times were lights left on in an unoccupied room? _____

     How many times was a TV, game console,

     or computer left on with no one using it? _____

Fig. 2: What temperature was the thermostat set to during the day?

Fig. 3: What was the lowest outdoor temperature at night?

3. For each day in your monitoring period, you will record your answers to a few questions listed on page 121. It will be handy to record these questions and responses in a log and keep them in a family-friendly spot for all to see and keep track of with tallies or responses (figs. 2 and 3). Or, you could discuss your responses as a group each day. As a tech-savvy option, you could also respond to each question in a spreadsheet or shared document for quick data analysis.

4. At the end of each week, look for any patterns or things that seem odd in your records. Were there any days when usage was higher or lower than others? If so what happened on those days that might explain the difference? What items could you do better with as a family?

5. Take the meter readings again at the close of each week. Subtract the first reading of the week from the final reading. This will equal your total energy consumption for the week. What hasn't been counted in the survey that is included in the meter reading? What items could be monitored more closely to use less of in upcoming weeks?

Smart Meters: There's an App for That!

An electric meter allows a utility company to keep track of a home's energy use. Electric meters help companies predict the amount of electricity they need to generate each day, and they also help companies know how much to bill us. Many utility companies are now replacing older meters with smart meters. These meters help consumers save money by allowing them instant access to their energy use through an app or online program. They can compare their use to the lowest user in their neighborhood and check for strange occurrences during the day. Utilities can also send alerts to customers that their energy use is high or that customers could save money by shutting off certain items. Some customers make agreements with their utility, allowing the company to turn down or shut off devices remotely at times of high demand (when everyone is using a lot of electricity). I guess Mom will know exactly when you're not doing your homework and hitting the video games!

ENERGY EXPLAINED

A typical family can spend around $2,000 on utility costs (electricity, heating, cooling, etc.) each year. If you monitor your consumption and find things that you can change through your family's behavior, or that you can change with a newer, more efficient technology, you might save money. Can you think of things you might put this money toward?

Utility bills can help your family keep track of energy use. Bills include information about how much energy was used during the month, how much was used in recent months, and what was used last year. Keeping track of these statistics can help your family identify the impact of each of conservation effort you make.

WASTE WATCHERS

TIME:
1 day

PERSON POWER:
No Sweat!

IMPORTANT NOTE:
You may want to complete this activity on a day you are around the house for a majority of the day.

"One man's trash is another man's treasure," a famous saying goes. How can trash be a treasure? We can do many things with the waste we generate each day: recycle, compost, landfill, burn it for energy, or reuse it. Everything that's given a new purpose is a treasure, because it can help provide energy, save money, or save our planet by using fewer resources. Does one person make enough trash each day to make a difference? Well, this lab will allow you to gather information about how much trash you produce!

Fig. 3: Put three colors of bingo chips or candies in a bag.

Fig. 1: Make a label for each of the trash bags.

Fig 2: Label each of the quart-sized bags.

📎 MATERIALS

→ **permanent marker**
→ **3 trash bags with ties**
→ **2 resealable, quart-sized plastic bags**
→ **bingo chips in 3 colors, or similar items like candy or coins**
→ **bathroom scale**

1. Use the marker to label each of your trash bags. Label one "Trash," one "Recycling," and one "Compost" (fig. 1). If you don't compost in your home or town, or if you don't have a garbage disposal for food waste, you can skip the third bag.

2. Use the permanent marker to write "Today's Trash" on one of the quart-sized bags (fig. 2). Mark the other bag "Chips" and put bingo chips of 3 colors in inside it (fig. 3). Assign one color of chip to coordinate with each of the trash bags. For example: Red chips = Trash, Green = Recycling, and Blue = compost. If you don't compost or use a garbage disposal, you may skip the third color of chips.

3. Carry both resealable bags around with you for the day. Anytime you generate some waste (food, paper, trash, empty containers, etc.) decide how to discard of each piece—trash, recycling, or compost. Take the waste to its proper trash bag and place it inside (fig. 4). Also, transfer a chip of the matching color into your Today's Trash bag (fig. 5). If you aren't at home, be sure you transfer the chip, but you don't have to carry the trash with you! Repeat this process all day, sorting out your garbage and keeping track.

Fig. 4: Put waste in its proper bag.

4. At the end of the day, take each of your trash bags to the scale and weigh it. Which kind of waste is the heaviest? Which kind of waste ends up taking up the most volume? How much total waste did you create?

5. Count the colored chips in your Today's Trash bag. Is the total for each color similar in proportion to the scale readings? Why or why not? Are some kinds of trash easier to deal with than others?

6. Check to make sure that the things in your recycling bag can all be recycled in your town, and place them in your home's receptacle. Do the same with the compost and trash.

Fig. 5: Transfer a chip to a bag.

PONDERING PLASTICS

Did you ever take a look at the bottom of a plastic bottle? There's always a recycling symbol with a number in it. What does the number mean? Plastics can be made in many shapes, sizes, and types. There are seven different types of plastics (including Styrofoam). Most are commonly recycled, and a few are not recycled. Each type is labeled with a number from one to seven inside the recycling symbol. This number is a code that tells consumers what each plastic is made from. Local waste-management groups can tell their communities which plastics they recycle by using these same codes. So check those labels!

ENERGY EXPLAINED

The average person typically generates at least 3 to 4 pounds of trash and recyclables each day! A little more than 50 percent of that goes to a landfill because many items cannot be recycled, were not properly sorted, or have little energy value.

About 10 percent of garbage is sent to facilities to be burned for electricity. In some cases, however, the landfilled waste is also used to generate electricity. In the landfill, as the waste decays, it releases methane gas. This gas has a high energy content and can be trapped and burned for electricity right on site. Methane gas builds up at a landfill and must be flared off to prevent fires or explosions, so why not burn it for electric power?

About 35 percent of the waste we create is recycled or composted. But not every town has the same facilities and regulations for recycling. Recycling materials saves space in landfills and can sometimes cut costs. However, it makes more sense to recycle some things than others, based the material they're made of, the energy content, and how much it costs to recycle them.

It makes a lot of sense to recycle glass, because it doesn't burn very well for energy and it doesn't break down easily. Steel and aluminum cans are great for recycling because the materials hold up over time and we can sometimes save 75 to 90 percent of the energy used to make new cans! Recycling plastics doesn't always make sense, however. It takes as much energy to recycle certain plastics as it does to make new items. In these cases, we often burn these materials at a trash-to-energy facility. Composting is used for yard waste and food scraps. We use the decay of these materials to create nutrient-rich material to mix with soil for farming and planting.

CARBONATION CONUNDRUM

TIME:
30 minutes, plus 2 minutes the night before (optional)

PERSON POWER:
No Sweat!

SAFETY IS KEY:
When using high-wattage bulbs, be sure to check the light fixture to make sure it is rated to support the wattage of the bulb. Ask an adult for help with this if necessary.

When we burn fossil fuels in our vehicles and in power plants, we release carbon dioxide molecules. Carbon dioxide exists in our environment naturally, but what happens if there is too much? How does carbon dioxide behave? This lab simulates how carbon dioxide behaves in relation to light and thermal energy (heat).

📎 MATERIALS

→ high-wattage, incandescent lightbulb (60 watt or higher, heat lamp, or work bulb)
→ clip lamp
→ 2 twenty-ounce soda bottles, unopened and of the same kind
→ ruler
→ push pin
→ sharp scissors
→ 2 digital kitchen thermometers
→ permanent marker

1. Make sure your lightbulb and lamp are compatible. Also, be sure the bulb you are using is an incandescent bulb. Heat lamp bulbs also work very well.

2. Open one of the bottles. Pour out about ⅓ of the soda (fig. 1). Re-cap the bottle tightly and shake it (fig. 2). Carefully open it and allow the fizz to dissipate. Repeat this process several times until most of the bubbles are gone. Put the cap on the bottle again.

Fig. 1: Open one of the bottles and pour out ⅓ of the soda.

3. Poke a pushpin into the bottle, just above the top of the label. Use the sharp scissors to make the hole slightly larger (fig. 3). Insert a digital thermometer into the hole (fig. 4). Remove the label from the bottle, and using your marker, label the bottle "Flat."

4. Remove the cap from the second bottle and pour out ⅓ of the soda so that it is about the same height as the first. *Do not shake* this

Fig. 2: Shake the bottle and allow the fizz to dissipate.

Fig. 3: Make a hole in the bottle.

Fig. 4: Insert the thermometer through the hole.

Fig. 5: Position the fizzy and flat bottles next to each other.

bottle. Return the cap and seal tightly. Remove the label and mark this bottle "Fizzy."

5. Poke a push pin into this bottle at roughly the same location as the first. Repeat the process to enlarge the hole and insert the digital thermometer.

6. Set your lamp just above the height of the bottles. Position the bottles next to each other, approximately 6" (15 cm) away from the lamp (fig. 5). Turn the bottles so that the thermometer screens face away from the light. Record the initial temperature of both bottles.

7. Turn on the lamp. Both bottles should be receiving equal amounts of light. Record the temperature of both bottles every two minutes for twenty minutes. What do you observe? Why aren't the temperatures the same?

ENERGY EXPLAINED

Carbon dioxide (CO_2) is a gas commonly found in nature. We exhale it when we breathe. When something is burned, CO_2 is released. Some items store carbon and carbon dioxide—the atmosphere, the ocean, animals, plants, and even fossil fuels. Burning fossil fuels releases CO_2, which moves into the atmosphere. When the atmosphere has too much of it, it warms up. But why?

Carbon dioxide is a greenhouse gas. Molecules of CO_2 act like the glass structure of a greenhouse. They allow in light as radiant energy which becomes thermal energy (heat) that can't get out. We call this the greenhouse effect, a process that helps keep the Earth warmer at night, when there's less radiant energy.

In this experiment, the bottles act like a greenhouse—the temperature inside it goes up when exposed to light.

The flat bottle has almost no CO_2. The fizzy bottle has more. You should have seen the fizzy bottle's temperature rise more than the flat bottle's due to the extra CO_2.

ROAD TRIP

When people talk about pollution and reducing our carbon footprint, they're asking us to consider our energy use. They want us to reduce the amount of carbon dioxide we contribute to the atmosphere with our activities. Well, how can we help? One way in which we as a society release the most carbon dioxide is through our day-to-day travels. In this lab, we will map a trip and determine just how much carbon dioxide we produce as we get from point A to point B.

Fig. 2: Consider a destination for your road trip.

TIME:
30 minutes to 1 hour

PERSON POWER:
No Sweat! But, you can always Grab a Crew Member! Math and imaginary road trips are always more fun with friends!

MATERIALS

→ atlas
→ Internet access
→ calculator
→ notebook and pencil

1. If you had to take a road trip, who would you take and what car would you use? Pick a car that holds the number of people you'd like to travel with (fig. 1). Go to www.fueleconomy.gov and record the year, make, model, miles-per-gallon (MPG) rating, and fuel type for the vehicle. What are some reasons you chose this vehicle?

2. Consider a destination for your road trip (fig. 2). Use the atlas or online map software to figure out the number of miles you would travel in a car to arrive there. Map your trip and record the total miles (fig. 3).

3. Make a list of the times you might stop and the towns or locations in which you will stop along the way (fig. 4).

Fig. 1: Pick a car that holds the right number of people.

Fig. 3: Map your trip.

Fig. 4: Make a list of the stops you will make.

4. How many gallons of fuel will you use? Divide the number of miles by the MPG rating of the car to figure out how many gallons of fuel you will need to drive to your destination.

5. How much does gasoline cost in your area? Multiply the number of gallons you will use by cost per gallon to estimate your trip cost.

6. What does your trip cost for the environment? Figure out how much carbon dioxide is released by your car by multiplying the number of gallons of fuel by the amount of CO_2 released per gallon. For a gasoline or flex-fuel vehicle, you will release 19.6 pounds (8.89 kg) of CO_2 per gallon (3.78 liters), and for diesel fuel, you will release 22.4 pounds (10.16 kg) per gallon (3.78 liters). (Figures taken from the United States Environmental Protection Agency (EPA).)

ENERGY EXPLAINED

Energy is required to transport us from place to place. In countries like the United States, the transportation of people and goods makes up a large chunk of energy use. Gasoline and diesel are made from petroleum, a fossil fuel, and must enter a combustion chamber in our vehicles. Combustion releases carbon dioxide, among other things. Transporting people in these vehicles is responsible for about one-third of the greenhouse gas emissions each year! We don't think much about the trips we take, but each gallon of gas adds up when we consider pollution and emissions. How could your next road trip reduce carbon dioxide and pollution or your carbon footprint? Energy-conservation behaviors like carpooling, using a bike or public transportation, or even walking can all help conserve resources, reduce carbon emissions, and preserve the environment.

GLOSSARY

Atom: The smallest particle that makes up all matter; everything is made from atoms

Centripetal force: A force that makes an object follow a curved path around a center point

Chemical energy: The energy stored within the chemical bonds of atoms and molecules. Chemical energy is found in the foods we eat and the fuels we use every day.

Chemical reaction: When two substances combine to form new substances, their chemical bonds are broken and new bonds are formed

Circuit: The path electricity follows

Compound: A substance made of more than one atom, held together with a chemical bond

Compost: A mixture that consists of decaying matter of once living things that is used for fertilizing land

Conductor: A material that allows heat or electricity to transfer through it

Ecosystem: A community of organisms that interact with their environment

Electricity: The movement of electrons in a circuit

Electrons: Parts of atoms that have a negative charge and create electricity

Endothermic: A reaction in which heat is released because more energy is created in the reaction than is needed to break bonds

Energy conservation: Saving energy by altering behaviors or choices

Energy efficiency: Saving energy by using technologies to do the same amount of work using less energy and costing less money overall

Exothermic: A reaction in which heat is absorbed from surroundings because more energy is needed to break bonds

Filament: A wire within a lightbulb that conducts electricity and has a high melting point. A filament will glow when electricity flows through it.

Friction: The force that opposes or pushes back against a moving object

Gravity: A force that attracts one body to another. On Earth, we are attracted, or pulled, to the ground, which is the center of gravity.

Inertia: A property that causes matter to resist a change in motion unless an outside force acts upon it

Insulator: A material that does not allow heat or electricity to pass through it

Kinetic energy: Energy in motion

Mass: The measure of an amount of matter in an object, measured on a scale or balance

Molecule: A group of atoms bonded together by the sharing or exchange of electrons

Nonrenewable: An energy source that is not able to be replenished as quickly as it is used

Nuclear fission: The process where neutrons in an atom are fissioned (split) to release energy for electricity in a power plant

Ore: A rock that contains valuable minerals or resources

Petroleum: A fossil fuel formed from the remains of ancient marine plant and animal organisms

Potential energy: Energy that is stored based upon its position or place

Protractor: A tool used to measure angles

Radiation: The movement of energy in waves

Radiant energy: Energy that travels in a wave or ray-like pattern, such as light, UV radiation, X-rays, radio waves, or microwaves

Reclamation: The process of returning used land to its original condition or better

Reflect: The throwing or casting back of wave energy, such as light, sound, or thermal energy, without it being absorbed

Refract: The bending of wave energy

Renewable: A source of energy that is able to be replenished quickly

Semiconductor: A material used in electronics to control the amount of energy used and heat produced

Thermal energy: The energy created by the friction of particles or materials rubbing against one another

Transparent: Allowing light to pass through so that objects can be seen

Utility: A company that is responsible for generating electricity or natural gas and transporting it to customers

Vibration: The back-and-forth motion of a body when it is disturbed

Viscosity: The property of a liquid to resist flowing or change in motion

RESOURCES

ALL THINGS ENERGY

www.need.org
www.eia.gov/kids
www.eia.gov/energyexplained
www.energy.gov
www.energy4me.org
https://phet.colorado.edu
www.nrel.gov
www.energy.gov/energysaver/energy-saver
www.fueleconomy.gov

ALL THINGS EARTH AND SPACE

www.nasa.gov
www.usgs.gov
www.noaa.gov
http://climatekids.nasa.gov

SCIENCE SUPPLIERS

Most of the activities can be completed using materials found in your local superstore, craft store, or home improvement store. For electronics or specialized equipment to further your experimentation, check out the following:
www.radioshack.com
www.flinnsci.com
www.stevespanglerscience.com
www.teachersource.com

INDEX

ACKNOWLEDGMENTS

THANK YOU to the NEED Teacher Advisory Board members, past and present, for testing, approving, and making energy education activities like those in this book successful and fun.

This book would not have been possible without the support of the NEED team in the office and in the field. Thank you for making energy education possible, rewarding, and exciting each and every day!

Judith Cressy and Meredith Quinn, thank you for your patience and encouragement in the writing and editing process.

Liz Heinecke and Amber Procaccini, thank you for willingly and beautifully capturing the fun and chaos in each of these experiments.

Thank you to all of the kids who got their hands dirty and found themselves energized by these labs!

ABOUT THE AUTHOR

EMILY HAWBAKER has always had energy and a passion for science and education. After graduating from Pennsylvania State University with a degree in Earth science and a minor in science education, Emily began teaching eighth grade science in Delaware County, Pennsylvania, not far outside of Philadelphia. Her school was chosen to take part in an energy education project, where students learned about their energy use and taught others about what they had learned with the help of the National Energy Education Development (NEED) curriculum and materials. Emily saw her students come alive with this program, and it fueled her own passion for energy education.

After several years, Emily left the classroom to join NEED full time as the curriculum director, where she works to edit activities, create new materials, and share her passion for energy education as a facilitator of teacher and student events and programming across the country and around the world. Emily even gets to see her old school every now and again! She loves seeing students and teachers alike have their a-ha! moments when learning about energy, and it keeps her going each day.

When Emily is not reading, writing, and workshopping, you can find her enjoying Philadelphia's sights and sounds, running, sailing, traveling, and tormenting her cats with a laser pointer.

ABOUT THE

THE NATIONAL ENERGY EDUCATION DEVELOPMENT (NEED) Project was established in 1980 as a nonprofit organization with a goal to promote an energy-conscious and educated society. NEED develops networks of students, educators, businesses, and government and community leaders to design and deliver objective, multi-sided energy education programs. NEED curriculum and training engages teachers and students in learning about energy in the world around them. Energy is fundamental to our daily lives, and it's important to understand it and its impact on each individual, as well as on the global community. NEED activities use a kids-teaching-kids approach to learning—students experiment, explore, research, and share their knowledge with their families, their peers, and their greater community. NEED aims to encourage students to become energy leaders today and tomorrow. For more information about NEED and its programming, curriculum, and student engagement efforts, visit www.need.org.

NEED

National Energy
Education Development

NEED PROJECT

Georgia John Mikaylah Maria Barrett Ayla Adem

Scarlett Cela Wyatt Grace Charlie Wyatt Gray

AJ Frankie Cady Kyra Sarah Carissa Nico

Max Alessa Mia Leo Sarah Elena Svea

Paavo Simon Isaac Anja Gwen Raya Emily

Lily Tessa Lili Annie Nora Ella Jaden

May Bridgett Nick Ava Ellie Carlo Harper